Gay Polarity Tantra

Volume 1

Nathaniel Reeves

Samarpan Alchemy Publications

Gay Polarity Tantra - Volume 1

© March 2015, Nathaniel Reeves

ISBN 978-1-907167-14-0

Published by:

Samarpan Alchemy Publishing
P.O. Box 813
Exeter
EX5 4WF
United Kingdom

Email: info@samarpan-alchemy.co.uk
Web: www.samarpan-alchemy.co.uk

Dedicated to:

Tom, with love (and something deep and meaningful in Latin). Sue K., Sue L. & Brenda, who acted as brilliant midwives for GPT.
And grateful thanks to Brian D. Parsons for publishing this book under his Samarpan Alchemy Publishing banner.

Contents

Part Four

Medical & Psychiatric Disclaimer:

The information contained in this book is aimed at resolving emotional, mental and spiritual issues, and is not intended to directly resolve physical and / or medical complaints and illnesses.

In all such cases, individuals are strongly advised to consult with a qualified medical practitioner about their physical condition.

If an individual is suffering from severe emotional and / or mental conditions, it is also strongly advised that they consult a qualified medical practitioner or other qualified mental health specialist.

Individuals should only use the information contained in this book in accordance with the laws and regulations of their country of residence.

Audio Essences, Crystal Holograms & Energy Cards:

In addition to crystal layouts, this book includes three additional ways to work with the techniques and processes contained within, namely:

- Audio Essences

- Crystal Holograms

- Energy Cards

More information on each of these unique methods can be found in Appendix C.

Real-Life Case Studies:

Many of the examples and case-studies contained in this book are drawn from real-life.

However:

- Wherever possible, permission for their inclusion has been obtained.

- Personal details have been changed to ensure that the privacy and anonymity of all the individuals is secured, without changing the meaning of the story itself.

PART ONE

Times change; are always slipping, shifting. Things that once were necessary, allowable, are not even possible any more because the energies and opportunities are no longer the same. Suddenly the directions of life have switched and a new path opens up for us ahead: full of obstacles to begin with but easier and easier for anyone to follow as soon as the first travellers have cleared the way. Before we know it, yesterday's impossiblity will be tomorrow's laziness.

Peter Kingsley

A Story Waiting to Pierce You

C1. Introduction:

It always starts with an idea.

Where the idea comes from you are never too sure... the Muses, from the Collective Unconscious, Divine Inspiration perhaps, or from the Past or even the Future? No one really knows for sure.

But somehow this idea gets inside your head, fights its way to the surface of your consciousness, and then makes enough mental noise to get noticed.

That is the point when the real journey starts. Because like any seed which touches the soil, growth, success and a long-life is not guaranteed, so many things can go wrong. For every tree that stands tall, there are many seeds and saplings which never 'make it'.

The same is true with new ideas. For example, does the human brain, which received this new idea, only notice it out of the corner of its eye, and then turn away, not even giving it a second thought? Maybe the human brain doesn't even notice the idea amidst all the mental chatter within its daily stream of consciousness, all competing for the brain's attention.

What if the idea is seen and understood? Is it actioned immediately... or disregarded as being silly, impractical, unworkable, too challenging, or ahead of its time? Or is it pushed to the back of the mind as something to consider 'later', and so the exact moment of divine inspiration is lost forever?

Many amazing ideas are lost this way, ideas which fall like rain... but land in the wrong brains, or during inconvenient times, and so never take root.

So what must happen for a new idea to take root within the human brain? Well, an individual who is fortunate enough to receive an original idea has to first give it space within their mind, and also allow it to intermingle and connect with other similar ideas, so that it can expand and start to take form. It is often not until two ideas meet and marry that a mental revolution really takes off... but this can only happen if the human brain has given these different ideas the space and permission to connect in the first place. And at the end of this alchemical process, the individual is left with one of two mental artefacts... either a **belief**... or a **theory**.

A belief is a number of inter-connected ideas that purport to explain how some aspect of the world works. Whether that belief is true or not is often of secondary importance. What is all important is that you believe in the belief, it helps to calm your mental anxiety, and helps you to fill in the gaps within your knowledge of the world around you... and so you start to mould your behaviour to fit in with your belief... even when that belief gets you into trouble with others and the world itself.

A belief is often a mental habit which we adopt because it makes our life easier, we don't have to make the effort to *think* each time a particular circumstance arises... we just allow our mental habit to kick in and control our response and behaviour.

However, a theory is a different beast entirely... although it is also composed of a number of inter-connected ideas. When you have a theory, you think you know how the world works... but you need to acquire hard evidence to prove it beyond reasonable doubt... and so this requires further work, investigation and information gathering.

In contrast, a belief is a 'done deal'. With a belief, you don't need to do any more research, because the belief tells you what to believe and think, even in the face of contradictory information and evidence. With a belief, you don't need to go searching for the truth because you already know it. If you don't believe me, try explaining a 100 million year old Dinosaur bone to a group of Creationists. In fact, if you wear your belief with total confidence, you may find other people start believing in it as well... as we all need something to believe in, and people may become envious of your confidence and certainty and want to buy into it.

But with a theory... well, it's different game entirely. With a theory, you can't say that you know, or that you have discovered the truth until you have uncovered the hard evidence to back up your theory... and even then you will probably have to write a scientific paper, which is then peer reviewed, published in a scientific journal, and generally accepted by the scientific community. You have to jump through a lot of academic hoops before the committee in Sweden awards you the Nobel prize... they don't give a Nobel out to just anybody. For example, Einstein published his Theory of General Relativity in 1905, and won the Nobel for Physics in 1921, sixteen years later. But he won the Nobel for his explanation of *the photoelectric effect*, and not for General or Special Relativity. Awarding him the Nobel for his Theory of Relativity was considered to be too politically controversial for the times.

So proving a theory takes time, commitment, patience, dedication, luck... and an open mind. Which are all the things which a great many people lack, which is why they choose to purchase a second-hand belief from their family, culture and society, rather than choosing to think and learn for themselves.

The thing is, with a theory, you can't afford to have a closed mind, even when you uncover evidence that contradicts your theory, because it just might open up a new door which takes your research in a new and more exciting direction. In this regards, open minds are like open doors... they open up new possibilities, they take you somewhere.

When you are working on a theory eventually you either discover it is 100% true, half-true, or you end up replacing it with something even better.[1]

It has been said that religions are based on *belief*, and science is based on *theory* and *the scientific method*. With an established religion, or newly founded cult, someone has to start it all off by claiming:

> *'I know the truth... No, I really mean it... God has told me... There is no need to look elsewhere for the truth because it's all been written down in this scripture for all time... There is no need to look for the truth elsewhere, because it is all here, everything you will ever need to live your life... just as long as you follow my God's rules.'*

In contrast, science starts with someone like Einstein publishing their theory in a scientific paper... and a lot of other scientists sitting around on mountain tops, gazing through powerful telescopes, looking for the evidence which will prove his theory (or blowing up nuclear bombs in the middle of a desert).

Anyone can come up with a *belief*, but it takes time, *effort* and collaboration to prove a theory.

Now in this book you are going to read about *Gay Polarity Tantra*. It started as an idea. Where it came from I am not entirely sure.

But somehow this idea got inside my head, fought its way up to the surface of my consciousness, and then made enough mental noise to get noticed. It pitched camp somewhere deep in my mind and started to meet-up with other ideas, formed friendships, alliances, love-affairs, started to expand and take form. And eventually it came back into my consciousness and presented itself to me as a **theory**. Not just a theory about the spiritual side of Gay sexuality, although this book is primarily written from a Gay perspective, but a theory

---

1   Unfortunately, not all scientists are open-mind, and it would be wrong to conclude that all religious followers are close-minded. Life isn't so black and white.

which is firmly embedded within the context of human sexuality and spiritual potential as a whole.

At this point, it is important that you realise that in this book I am not trying to sell you a second-hand belief system, but I am attempting to put the meat and bones on a theory.

So as you read this book, you will discover:

- A new theory about the spiritual nature of human sexuality.

- A new theory about how Gay sexuality, male and female, sits within that broad spectrum of possible human sexual expression.

- Evidence which I currently 'believe' supports this theory.

- All of which are supported by practical techniques / processes that you can try yourself to prove whether the theory works for *you*, coming in later volumes.

The 20th century mystic Osho said that he never formulated systems to explain how the inner consciousness of man worked, he only gave clues and hints about the inner nature of consciousness.

Why? Because he felt that if you gave someone an entire system ready-made then they would only start 'believing in it' and this very belief would stop their own investigations of their inner world. If you already think you know how something works, why bother to explore further? Whereas, if you gave someone clues and hints it was much more likely that they will act on them, if only out of curiosity, and start off down the inner trail, making their own spiritual discoveries along the way to their eventual enlightenment.

Unfortunately, this is indeed the fate of many, many religious followers... following the religious leader's original insights and discoveries, hoping that just by following scripture to the letter will automatically deliver them to heaven, salvation, moksha, nirvana, and enlightenment. But enlightenment is what we 'achieve' for ourselves alone, not something we can ever acquire, purchase, or borrow from others.

This is why I don't want anyone to assume that everything in this book is 100% correct... because I don't want you to start *believing in it*. In my ideal world, I want my readers to take this information and start thinking about it, testing it, trying it on for size, adjusting it to fit their particular circumstances if necessary... to start living it. Because this is the way to not only prove, but also to *transform yourself within*... which is the ultimate proof possible in this Universe of ours. You become the proof and express it through your life... and it's so much better than just *believing*.

And the practical clues you will find in this book, and also in *Gay Polarity Tantra* Volume 2 which is available as a free PDF download (refer to Appendix C for more about how to access), should hopefully make this inner process of discovery easier.

My hope is that this book gives Gay people:

• The realisation that there is a way to express their innate sexuality in a spiritual way, and not to buy into what Straight Tantrics and religious fanatics say about Gay people and their potential (i.e. people who usually haven't a *clue* but who definitely have an *agenda*... much, much more on this later).

• A map to set people off in the right direction, and the courage to explore within.

• And the inner confidence to realise that as far as God / the Universe / the Tao is concerned, there is nothing wrong with Gay people, and God / the Universe / the Tao gave us all a spiritual birth right that is just waiting to be claimed... it's just a matter of *looking in the right place*.

C2. Squaring the Circle:

This is a book that describes a possible path of Tantra for Gay people, both male and female.

Now, from the outset, we need to be clear that this book *does not*:

> • Describe or contain a range of different sexual positions or physical techniques available for Gay people.

> • Explore and discuss, at any great length, the views which different religions and spiritual traditions have towards homosexuality.

Both of these topics are outside the scope of this book.

So if you are looking for that sort of thing, it will be best to look elsewhere, and there are several books which do cover these areas.

So if this book isn't about any of those topics... what is it about? Well, it is an exploration of sexual energy and polarity from a 'Gay perspective'. Because the central question at the heart of Gay Tantra, the question of whether or not it is possible or feasible, is primarily one of 'energy' and 'polarity'.

This is why the book is entitled *Gay Polarity Tantra*, and the issue which lies at the heart of Gay Polarity Tantra can best be understood through the quote below, which is drawn from Bruce Frantzis Kumer's book *Taoist Sexual Meditation: Connecting Love, Energy and Spirit*:

> *The ultimate purpose of Taoist spiritual sexuality involves two partners creating a combined third central channel. This can only be achieved by a man and a woman, just as a man and a woman are necessary to make a physical*

*baby. The Taoist system of sexual meditation was designed
to specifically utilize the combination of yin and yang to
create an alchemy that enabled deep spiritual growth to
manifest. Outside this tradition, there may be exoteric
sexual practices that are deemed quite suitable for same-
sex partners; however, these are outside the scope of this
book.[1]*

The question of whether there are 'esoteric sexual practices' for Gay
individuals / same-sex partners *is* within the scope of *this* book.

It's what this book is *all* about. It includes, brings together and draws
upon all that I have read, discovered, explored, and sometimes even
'tripped over' during the first 50 years of my life. Information I have
found to be useful, beneficial, life-saving, unusual, unexpected...
and sometimes information that flies totally against the traditional
and conventional stream of thought... but which seems to work
nonetheless.

Now I have always thought and believed somehow that the real
question of whether Gay Tantra is possible or not depends on solving
this issue of 'polarity', of how the energy sets up between two Gay
individuals, whether male or female. Fundamentally, it is a question
of *Yin* and *Yang*.

Traditional Tantra and Taoist spiritual sexology have models that
describe how energy sets up between a Straight man and woman,
and these models have been very successful over the centuries for
heterosexual couples within those cultures and spiritual traditions.
But these same traditions do not include information on how
beneficial, healing energy can be set-up between two Gay men or
two Gay women.

In fact, these traditions most often suggest that it is *impossible* for two
Gay men, or two Gay women, to create and share beneficial, spiritual

---

1   Bruce Frantzis Kumer, pages 418-419.

sexual energy.

The argument goes that only a male / female couple can sexually create a point of balance and harmony between Yin and Yang. If two Gay men try then they will end up being too Yang, and if two Gay women try they will be too Yin. Both sets of Gay couples are believed to be too inherently imbalanced to create a harmony between Yin and Yang... and to attempt so will be dangerous to themselves.

But...

I have also somehow known, deep within, that it **is** possible for a Gay couple to create such a point of balance and harmony... it was just a question of finding how... or of the Tao deciding that it was time for it to be discovered... or re-discovered, depending upon your point of view.

Part of the reason why I believe such a system of Gay Tantra doesn't currently exist is because Gay people need to develop and create for *themselves* a theory / model which best describes how their *own* energies work... A theory / model that allows them to use their own sexual energies for personal and spiritual development... But also a theory / model that does not negate the Straight model, but extends it in a new direction.

Now to be fair, there are several books on Gay Tantra currently on the market, and many of these have made a positive contribution to the debate. But personally, I do not believe anyone to date has put forward a credible theory / model which answers / solves the question of how the Yin / Yang polarity works for Gay people.

To date, I believe we have just been trying to adapt Straight Tantra into something that will fit / work for Gay people. The problem with doing that is you are still playing on the Straight Tantra 'pitch', with their 'ball', and subject to their 'rules'. We have been trying to square the circle, without realising that circles are not squares, and never will be... so why try to change them?

Time after time, Gay people who practice a form of Tantra come up against the same old argument... Gay men are too Yang... Gay women are too Yin... it's not going to work.

However, the reason why I like the Bruce Frantzis Kumer quote, and have included it at the start of this book, is that at least he's being *honest*. He's kind of saying Gay Tantra may be possible... but you're not going to find it over here with us... you're going to have to work it out for yourselves.

What if the solution to the polarity issue for Gay people means that Gay Tantra turns out to be something *radically different*.... something that the Straight Tantra community couldn't even possibly conceive of in a thousand years (because it is so 'outside the box'). If that is the case, we will need a new, bigger, and more inclusive model of how Yin and Yang manifest through heterosexual *and* homosexual couples.

Historically that is exactly how science works. A scientist puts forwards a theory to describe phenomenon 'A', and because their theory can not only successfully describe phenomenon 'A', but can also be proven repeatedly through experimentation, or can successfully predict when phenomenon 'A' will occur, other scientists eventually get together and decide that this theory is *correct*, and will start referring to it as a law. They may even award the scientist the Nobel prize for being super-clever in their particular field.

But later, a pesky young scientist comes along and says 'Well, what about phenomenon 'AB'... our existing theory doesn't describe that... it doesn't seem to be able to predict that... I believe we need a new theory to describe what is going on'.

Then, either the original theory is thrown out completely, or it is replaced by something better, or it is modified a little so that it can include 'A' and 'AB'.

Basically, that's how names and reputations are made in the big, bad, crazy world of science.

Actually, it's usually not as straightforward as that. Often the young scientist is ridiculed, picked on, thrown out of their scientific organisation or club, no one will publish their research papers for fear of 'contamination by association'... Until years later, all the old guard have either retired, or died, and the new 'establishment' can no longer ignore the evidence stacking up in favour of the 'new' theory. I was also going to say that if someone can make money out of the new idea, then that process is usually speeded up. But then I remembered the life of Nikolai Tesla, and realised that's not always true either. For a group of people who claim to only work with 'hard proof' and 'cold reason', scientists can also be very 'prejudiced' and 'irrational'. But... can't we all?

So this is where I am suggesting we currently are with the development of a form of Tantra relating to Gay people.

There is an existing model, written by Straight people, to describe how energy and polarity works... and it is a very successful model... for *them*. But it doesn't include a workable section on how the energy and polarity works for Gay people. And why should it, because Straight people probably won't understand how the energy of Gay people works, and why would they develop something which isn't going to be useful for them anyway?

Because of this, the Straight Tantra people argue 'Well, you Gay guys don't fit into our model... *So there has to be something wrong with you*... It's obviously not *our* model which is at fault, because it works for us... So it must be *you* who are in error... So we've decided we're just going to ignore you and pretend you don't exist... So just go in the corner, be quiet, and don't disturb our beautiful meditation space.'

Therefore, it is now over to the Gay crowd to play the role of the 'pesky, young scientist' and come back with...

> "Well, we respect your theory... and we understand that it works for you Straight people... But you have to understand that it doesn't work for us... So we're going to modify and broaden the model a little so that it does indeed work for us Gay people as well."

Now, the Straight Tantra community may reject what is in this book, they may be afraid that we're trying to trash their nice, tidy model, and they may try and keep Gay people out of their communities...[2]

If the information in this book means, as a result, a number of Gay people live more happy, fulfilled and spiritual lives... then, personally, I don't really give a shit what Straight Tantra thinks. Straight Tantra has been keeping Gay people out of their temples for centuries, so what they do think, or don't think, isn't going to make much difference now.

So a lot rests on this new theory which we shall be exploring throughout the rest of this book. Whether it is right or wrong will be determined by whether it is more successful at describing how the energy and polarity successfully sets up for Gay individuals and couples, which is why during this book we will spend time explaining the theory in some detail (but hopefully in an easy to understand way).

But the theory also has a lot of interesting things to say about Straight men and woman, how their energies work together, and also how Gays / Straights interact energetically... because as this theory has developed it has taken me into some very interesting places, and

---

2   Although, after reading this book, you may come to the conclusion that because Straight Tantra and Gay Tantra are so 'different', there isn't much point in entering anyway.

produced some unexpected insights and conclusions.

This book is primarily being written from the perspective of Gay people, male and female... to provide the understanding and techniques which they need for their own spiritual development.

There is something else which Bruce Frantzis Kumer once wrote, which I believe is very useful for our consideration at this point. He basically said that when engaging in sexual practices, you should never confuse the different levels of intention. (The spiritual teacher Duane Packer would call it being 'level appropriate'.)

For example, sexual energy can be used for:

- Creating babies, continuing the species

- Having fun

- Healing

- Meditation

- Spiritual Development

So if you are trying to conceive a baby, but are using techniques designed for sexual meditation, you may not end up with the result that you want (and vice versa)![3]

If we look at this from the perspective of Gay Men and Women, the first intention doesn't really apply (unless a Gay man and woman are getting together specifically to create a baby... which is anatomically possible).

If Gay Polarity Tantra does work, then all the remaining four

3   Although there is always the possibility that you may end up with a very spiritual baby!

intentions will therefore still apply for Gay people.

However, when using the information contained in this book, you will have an easier time if, from the start, you are clear and honest about your intentions. So if you want to utilize the techniques contained in the later sections of this book just for Fun, then there is nothing wrong with that. But don't then confuse or delude yourself into believing that you are engaging in some form of meditation, because if that were true your focus will need to change as you move from level to level... even if the basic energy set-up remains the same.

The same is also true for healing. If I am correct (and at this early stage of the book, that is still a *Big If* that I will need to prove to your satisfaction), then Gay people can also use these techniques for energy healing. But if you are engaging in Gay Tantra for healing, either for yourself, or your partner, then this will once again require a different focus, and so you need to be clear about that. Overall, the process becomes easier if you can remember to be clear about your intent, and also the intent of your partner if you have one, because things are easier if you are *both* heading in the same general direction. If you are both in disagreement, then I suggest you start with Fun and see what happens / evolves over time. You can always decide to change your intent later on, if or when your priorities change, but it is always best to have set an intent for each stage of your journey, because it makes things easier to manage.

This brings us to the other important element of this book. This book isn't just a book about *theory*. If it was, it would still contain lots of useful information. But it is not.

I could have written this as a theory book, and withheld the practical information, so no one could ever argue that, based on their direct experience, this theory is wrong.

But where is the fun in that?

Therefore, this is a book which also aims to provide Gay people with the foundation for practical ways to prove, in their own lives, whether this theory is or is not correct. (The Volume 2 free PDF will then contain the first of set of practical techniques, as it wasn't possible to fit everyting into one book at this time.)

Eventually every theory has to be put to the test to see if it is right. For example, some modern physicists do not like Superstring Theory because, by its very nature, there is no experiment which can ever be done which proves whether the theory is right or not. So it is an intellectual ivory tower. Very pretty to look at, but no one can ever prove whether it is real or an illusion.

But anyone who really knows me will support that I am not one for building ivory towers. I am much more interested in things which can make a real difference to people's lives. Which is what I am trying to do here. So if you do decide to download Volume 2, you will be given practical ways to explore this model for yourself... and these practical tools will be applicable to those people who are in a relationship... and also to those who are currently single... to Gay men and Gay women. I will even include techniques for those Gay individuals who want to develop their internal energies, but are not interested in doing so through the use of sexual energy (...and yes, those kinds of people do exist).

Now I cannot guarantee that these techniques will work for everyone. Nothing works for everyone. But in amongst the different techniques and processes on offer, I hope that you can find one thing that does indeed click with you.

These techniques are not limited to the energy system of one single tradition. I will include ways to work with the meridian system, the extraordinary vessels, and the chakra system. By doing this, I hope to have included something which resonates with you.

Also, as these energy techniques do not belong to any specific religion or existing spiritual tradition, and so you should be able to easily work with them, regardless of the spiritual belief system you currently adhere to. Along the way, we'll be including information which also helps to put Gay Polarity Tantra into some kind of historical and cultural context, because, as someone once said, if you don't know where you have come from, how can you work out where you are going?

This book does require you to be open-minded, and it does require you to be open to the possibility that you are much more than just your physical body. If you currently rigidly believe that you are just a physical body, and that when you die, that's it... then you may have a problem with most of the information contained in this book.

Although if you do keep reading, and later do some of the energy techniques on offer... you never know... you may be pleasantly surprised... This book has been written mainly for a Gay readership, but there is much to interest those in the Straight Tantra community with open minds, so I would not try to dissuade you from continuing reading on.

Finally, a story which I love, told by the 20th Century mythologist, Joseph Campbell.

Back in the late 1960s, a religious conference was held, bringing together representatives from the world's main religious and spiritual traditions – Christian, Islam, Jewish, Hindu, Buddhist etc. The aim of this conference was to discover if there were common themes amongst all these different traditions, things they could all agree on, and which could be used to build lasting peace between the different religions of the world.

Very soon the conference divided into two camps. But, interestingly, the division between these two camps was not based on ideological differences... It was based on *experience*.

On one side there were all those whose 'knowledge' only came from scripture and text, and so they sat around for hours, arguing over every last detail, about which tradition was right, and which was wrong, how many angels could dance on the head of a pin etc.

On the other side were all the people who actually engaged in regular meditation, in prayer, in some form of spiritual practice. And when these people met, they very soon realised that, even though they were all following different spiritual traditions, they had all had similar *inner experiences*.

As the saying goes, no matter where you stand in the world, the ocean always tastes salty. For these people, although they had followed different traditions, they had all journeyed within and experienced the same *source*. And because of that, these people soon realised that, because they had so much in common, they had no need to argue.

So remember... If your 'knowing' is just theory, then there is always the fear that it may be wrong, there is always doubt at the back of your mind, and there is always the need to argue with others to prove, to them and yourself, that you are 'right'. But when your 'knowing' comes from direct experience, then you truly know, and this wisdom is yours for life... in fact, it becomes something you can build your life upon. And who wants to waste time arguing anyway?

Final Word:

Ways of practically working with sexual energy can be found in many of the world's esoteric spiritual systems.

In the Hindu and Buddhist systems it is known as *Tantra*, in China it is often referred to as *Taoist Sexology*, and there are even systems found in amongst the different Native American tribes.

Within these distinct traditions, there are also a number of different schools, each with their own beliefs, techniques and practices. But for the purposes of this book, we are going to roll all of this spiritual and cultural diversity up into a single word – i.e. 'Tantra'.

This is done, not as a sign of disrespect to any of those established traditions and their differences, but as a way of simplifying the process of communicating what can be a complex and confusing subject.

Unfortunately, in the West, popular culture has come to associate Tantra with some kind of 'sexual practice'... with or without the attachment of a spiritual goal. However, someone once estimated that only 15% of Hindu and Buddhist Tantra relates to actual sexual practices... while the remaining 85% has nothing whatever to do with sexual energy.

What is interesting is that Gay Polarity Tantra works with or without the input or sexual energy... although this book probably puts greater emphasis on the sexual side, as opposed to the non-sexual side. But for anyone out there who feels that I am painting traditional Tantra in too narrow a way, I offer my sincere apologies. This was not done to show disrespect, or out of ignorance.

When you are writing a book such as this, you have to make choices, and you have to decide what it the best route to take for the majority of your readership. The way this book has been written, and the information which it contains, reflects the choices I have made along the way. Any mistakes made because of this are mine and mine alone, and I accept responsibility for them.

C3. Potential for Gay Tantra:

Over the past 20 years, whenever I have picked up and read a book on Tantra written by Straight authors, what they have had to say about Gay people has fallen into one of the following four categories:

1. The book has absolutely *nothing* to say about Gay People within the context of Tantra, and it is as if Gay people do not exist.

2. The authors take the view that Gay sexuality is wrong, immoral and unnatural, and that Gay people are basically 'malfunctioning' human beings, whose best bet is to pray that they are reborn heterosexual in their next lifetime, or engage in some kind of reconstructive psychology in this, their current life.

3. The book acknowledges that Gay people *do* exist, is actually very supportive, but because it was written by Straight people for Straight people, unfortunately it doesn't have the time to discuss Tantra from the perspective of Gay people. But there usually is the suggestion that Gay people can always 'adapt' the Straight techniques to better fit their needs.

4. The authors are 'kind of' supportive towards Gay people, but then state that because Gay sexuality doesn't fit Yin / Yang polarity theory, engaging in Gay Tantra will only lead to an energy 'imbalance' which will be positively dangerous for the Gay people practicing it (men more than women).

Now, there is a fifth type of Tantra book, which has been written by Gay people for Gay people, which is usually very supportive and inclusive. These types of book are brilliant on the applications and positions etc., but they usually don't provide a workable solution for the whole polarity issue. When I read any of the first 4 Straight types of Tantra book, what I feel personally is that:

1. To write a book on Tantra and not include at least one single paragraph on 10% of the human population is just *wrong*, but this is what this first type of book does... maybe because the author doesn't know any Gay people, or doesn't feel comfortable writing about them. But it shows that, as Tantric practitioners, they don't get out much. The percentage figure quoted for the number of homosexuals in any human population is usually 10%, although some lower it to 3% for Gay men and 2% for Gay women. However, I have reason to believe it is somewhere around 8% for both. But for the purposes of this text I am going to go with 10% because it makes the maths easier.

2. To argue that homosexuality is wrong on moral grounds is usually quite 'dodgy'... because what is morally *good* or *bad* is usually a culturally specific thing, having a limited time span. What is morally acceptable for one culture may not be acceptable for the one next door. Or the one which comes into existence one hundred years later.

I have always wondered what will happen when all the Christians finally get to heaven. Will their shared 'belief' be enough to merge them into one, big happy family, or will they be so different that they'll be at each other's throats?

For example, a Christian living in the 1st Century A.D. would have a very different set of attitudes and beliefs to an individual living in the Middle Ages, and to another individual living in the late 20th Century... and that is even before you take different churches, sects and dominations into consideration. If you did manage to get them all together in the same room, and they compared their beliefs and interpretation of scripture, then you might conclude that they weren't even practicing the same religion.

All you have to do is open the Bible at Leviticus and read through the list of crimes which, thousands of years ago, you would have been stoned by your fellow believers for committing... but which now are a part of our everyday life. Even Christians are now wearing garments made of two different threads!

Basically, moral rights and wrongs change over time... are mainly a reflection of the popular prejudices of the dominant culture... and most often lack any independent or scientific basis... despite what the believers would argue to the contrary. But then, we could say the same for any religion.

3. The approach which says 'Well, we haven't got time to discuss your particular needs in this book, just adapt the techniques to suit your requirements'... I think this is another cop out. It assumes that the needs of Gay people are basically the same as Straight people ...which I am going to argue in this book that they are *not*... but even if they *are* then it still leaves Gay people alone, having to figure everything out for themselves. That to me is a bit like trying to assemble a flat-pack, self-assembly bookcase where someone has forgotten to give you the instructions. Just 'making it up as you go along' doesn't always produce a stable or good-looking bookcase.

If the needs of Gay people are radically different from Straight people, then it leaves them totally 'screwed', because they'll be trying to figure out a viable route, using a map that is sending them in completely the *wrong direction*.

There is an assumption that Gay Tantra will be 'similar' to Straight Tantra, although with different diagrams. But I honestly do not believe that is the case. They are, and need to be, very different. And if they are different, then expecting Straight people to have discovered the principles and practices of Gay Tantra is about the same as expecting a group of monkeys, who are bashing away on the keys of typewriters over a million years, to have accidentally produced the complete works of Shakespeare.

4. As for the question of what is and is not 'natural'... well, we'll cover that in the next chapter.

I have always believed that the Universe / God / Tao is fundamentally *compassionate*, and it wouldn't create Gay people... and keep on creating them... if there wasn't a *reason*...if there wasn't also a way for Gay people to return to Source and achieve enlightenment... And if there is such a path Gay people need to find it for themselves... although I also believe that a compassionate Universe will have left 'clues'.

But the question of Yin / Yang theory is the real, stumbling block. Because you can ignore cultural dictats, you can overlook what is meant to be natural / unnatural... you can even turn a blind eye to how Straight people believe Gay people should behave. But you can't ignore physics, chemistry, biology... and subtle energies. You can't ignore how the Universe is put together.

For example, I can believe all the positive stuff I want, say the right affirmations until I am blue in the face... But if I then stick a finger into an electrical socket, I am going to get burned, and all my inner work and chanting won't protect me.

That's how electricity is. I either learn to work with it, safely, or I get burnt.

So, if Yin / Yang polarity is the issue... just believing we are Gay and we're OK, won't stop us from getting burned by the energies if we are using them *incorrectly*. Unless...

We arrive at new and deeper understanding of these energies... and learn to work with them, safely... rather than against them... And this is really what this book is all about... So let's keep going.

C4. The Natural World:

One of the things which is continually being thrown at Gay people is that *'It's not natural...'*

Hence, the classic image of a farmer saying, 'Well, I don't see my pigs, chickens and cows doing 'it', so it can't be natural... so it's wrong... it's *not* God's law!' Now, why a group of animals which have been domesticated by man for over 6,000 to 7,000 years should be considered the gauge for the rest of the natural world is something beyond me... but let's run with their argument for the moment.

> *If it doesn't happen in the natural world, if God's creatures don't do it, then it must be unnatural.*

However, one of the biggest arguments to the contrary, and so the greatest step forwards in our understanding of 'Gayness' in the last 50 years has come.... not from psychologists and psychiatrists... but from wildlife documentary filmmakers and zoologists, who have actually gone out into wild nature and documented what is *really going on*.

They have learnt that nature isn't as uniform, or as 'straight', as your average fundamentalist would like to believe. In fact, if the fundamentalists ever realised what is really going on just outside of their backdoor, they'd probably be out decimating 'deviant nature' with machetes and flamethrowers... And your argument that 'But God made it that way...' probably wouldn't go down too well either. Their version of God definitely *did not create that*, and you will not change their minds no matter what kind of contrary evidence you present to their sweet, angelic faces.

So let's engage with a fundamentalist for a moment, theoretically speaking, and see what happens.

US: So, you are a fundamentalist, and believe that Gay people are wrong because gay sex doesn't happen in nature, right?

FUNDAMENTALIST: Yes, I believe that human beings should only do what God intended, and if it doesn't happen in nature then it's not natural.

US: Ok then… So it is alright for women to kill men after sex and eat them?

FUNADAMENTALIST: What! No!

US: But that's what happens in nature. Some female spiders will eat the male of their species after sex, because they are a ready food source, and this helps them and their spider lings to survive. The same thing happens with mantises as well.

FUNADAMENTALIST: No, of course not, that's not what I meant. Anyway, that's insects. I didn't mean insects.

US: OK, no insects… So it's OK for women to dominate men.

FUNADAMENTALIST: No! Why do you say that?

US: Well, there are many varieties of birds where the female is dominant, and the male is completely subservient. So if your argument is that we should only do what is 'natural', then we should take that as a blueprint for human behaviour maybe? So your wife should be in charge of the finances…and maybe you should be obeying her more?

FUNADAMENTALIST: No! That's birds. Look, when I mean

'natural' I am referring to mammals, not birds or insects.

US: Well, we have dolphins which engage in homosexual relations?

FUNADAMENTALIST: No, that's fish... I said mammals!

US: Well, technically, dolphins are mammals... Never mind... We'll stick to mammals to keep you happy. Well, wolves have been observed to engage in homosexuals acts with other members of their own pack.

FUNADAMENTALIST: Look, when I said mammals, I meant mammals walking on two legs, like we do, great apes, monkeys, those sort of creatures... not wolves who walk on four legs.

US: OK, two legs it is then... Well, chimpanzees have been observed to engage in homosexual practices, and they're the closest relatives we humans have in the natural world, evolutionary speaking.

FUNADAMENTALIST: Well, I don't believe in evolution, it's too communist... And animals only behave like that in in zoos!

US: No, they have been observed engaging in homosexual acts in the wild as well, and...

And this is the point where the fundamentalist probably thumps you for being *too right*... or does something worse.

If human beings could be persuaded to change just through the power of rational argument and clear headed debate then the world really would be a different place.

Now, the point of this section isn't to teach you how to win an argument against a fundamentalist or close minded bigot. If you try, you'll lose, because it's not a matter of having the right facts or the most persuasive arguments. People like that will always refuse to think outside their mental prison, to let go of their narrow view of reality, because they have too much invested in it on an ego level. My advice is *don't even try*, as it's a complete waste of time and energy. They only want to hear what they already believe to be true.

Instead, the point is to show Gay people that the whole *"If it doesn't happen in the natural world, if God's creatures don't do it, then it must be unnatural"* argument just doesn't hold water, because we now know that Mother Nature doesn't behave in the way which fundamentalists think she does... and if your average fundamentalist ever discovered what is going on 'out there' in nature it would make them very, very uncomfortable.

Just because a farmer works with animals, doesn't give him a full understanding of how nature actually works, and scripture was usually written by prophets who, although they may have been well acquainted with the spiritual dimensions of life, were definitely not experts on the natural world.

One of the great mistakes that humanity has ever made is to assume that just because someone is enlightened, although this makes them a Master of their own Self, it doesn't automatically make them a master of 'anything else'... like personal finance, motor car maintenance, fine-art forgery, French cuisine, or the behaviour of wild animals.

I mean, Gautama the Buddha *did* meditate out in the forests, surrounded by nature. But while he was meditating, he kept his eyes firmly *closed*, and so he couldn't *see* the naughty goings on of the animals all around him. So how can he be considered the world's pre-eminent naturalist? Gautama the Buddha is known for developing *The Middle Way* and *4 Noble Truths*, not for writing *The Origins of the Species*. To be honest, I don't think the ancient Straight

Tantrics and Taoists were really paying that much attention to the real 'reality' of nature either. To understand how animals really interact requires you to focus in on that subject, to dedicate your life to it, and the serious science of Zoology has only been around for 300 years at most. Anyone practising zoology before then was doing so as a hobby, lacking little or any formal training or scientific discipline.

However, the fundamentalists can always fall back on their final, killer argument, which is 'Those animals are engaging in those homosexual acts because the Devil put them up to it!'

But these are the same fundamentalists who argue that only man has a Soul, which is why they are allowed to be so horrible to their fellow creatures, over which God has given man dominion. But if animals have no Soul, why would the Devil go to so much trouble to corrupt them and ensnare them into committing sin? Surely he would have better things to do with his time? If animals can fall into sin, shouldn't good Christians be out in the forests trying to save as many animals as possible, domesticated and wild, by baptising them and welcoming them into the fellowship of Christ? To me, it just doesn't make sense… but when has rational sense ever got in the way of fundamentalist thinking and a good, old-fashioned prejudice.

And what would happen if the Catholics and Protestants started to argue over who had converted the same squirrel? Basically, the whole thing would be completely unworkable… and some might argue that that is as a good definition of organised religion as any. Now, if you think I am being a bit silly here, I would point out that there is a department in the Mormon Church, based in Salt Lake City, whose job it is to convert all the people who have ever existed throughout history (a back-dated conversion, obviously), in order to save their Souls from eternal damnation. I am not making this up, that's what they do, 7 hours a day, 5 days a week, saving all the Souls throughout history without their ever knowing. However, I would imagine this will make the Last Day of Judgement a bit confusing when billions of Sikhs, Jains, Buddhists, Muslims, Taoist, Hindus, and various shamanic hunter-gatherers find themselves in Mormon heaven all of a sudden, with no clear idea of how they got there.

It's only when documentary cameramen / zoologists started filming various animals species up close and personal, that we started to see what is really going on in nature. And it isn't all tidy, straight, vanilla, heterosexual encounters. In a B.B.C. natural world documentary, called *Animals in Love* (2015), it was stated that so far scientists have documented 450 animal species who engage in homosexual activity… and that is probably just the tip of the iceberg.

This is in captivity *and* in the wild, between male *and* female members of the same species. Also, one of the arguments has always been that animals only engage in homosexual activities if they are denied a mate of the opposite sex. But scientists have now found that this argument also doesn't completely hold water, because pair-bounded, homosexual 'animals' will continue with their Gay partnership, even though they could split up and breed with one of any newly introduced mates of the opposite sex. Apparently, love is more powerful than sex for many species.

Only one of those 450 species has been known to actively persecute homosexual members of their own species… any guesses for which one that maybe? The other 449 species seem to have better things to do with their precious time.

If you want to know more about this area, read either of these two excellent books:

- Bruce Bagemihl's *Biological Exuberance: Animal Homosexuality and Natural Diversity* (University of California Press, 2009).

- Joan Roughgarden's *Evolution's Rainbow: Diversity, Gender and Sexuality in Nature and People* (St. Martin's Press, 1999).

Although I warn you, they are both big, heavy, academic reads.

But if you do need more hard evidence to help you delete the whole, 'homosexual = unnatural' argument from your head, then they will provide you with barrel loads of information to help you achieve this. So when you hear someone say that being Gay *"Just isn't natural,"* hopefully, you can know think to yourself, *"But what is?"*

Because the bottom line is:

• Nature is **not** filled with only 100% polite, safe, committed heterosexual partnerships.

• Nature **does** contain homosexual partnerships, across the whole of the animal kingdom.

And as Cole Porter would say:

Birds do it, Bees do it, Even educated fleas do it, Let's do it...
Let's fall in love...

C5. Morality & Culture:

We live at a very, very interesting time in human history.

In fact, the political British journalist Andrew Marr, in his B.B.C. series *History of the World* states that the most interesting time in human history is 'just around the corner'... how our human race copes with the mounting challenges of the 21st Century. One of the things about being a human alive 'right now' is that we are living at a time when 'cultures are colliding'.

As Sting sings in his song *Send Your Love*:

> *This is the time of the worlds colliding*
> *This is the time of kingdoms falling*
> *This is the time of the worlds dividing*
> *Time to heed your call.*

It's a bit like the movement of the tectonic plates across the surface of the planet. But instead of each plate being composed of rock and stone, floating on a sea of red hot magma, these *cultural plates* are instead composed of belief and prejudice, floating on a sea of red hot intolerance, and they move a lot faster.

Right now, Western culture is colliding headlong with the Middle Eastern / Islamic culture... and sometime over the next century there is bound to be multiple 'collisions' with the Chinese culture as it starts to 'shift' around the planet. When these different cultures collide, there can be violent *belief-quakes*... or where the fabric of society is ripped apart by erupting volcanos of hate and anger. Unfortunately, the process is seldom smooth or peaceful.

You could argue that this is a good thing because, for thousands of years, cultures have been able to continue, in isolation and unchallenged, with beliefs and attitudes which promote the persecution of individuals and groups within those cultures. It is only in the last couple of centuries that, generally through the expansion of Western culture and commerce, across the globe, societies have come into contact with, and been challenged by, beliefs and attitudes which are not their own.

For example, in Madagascar there are tribes who still consider the birth of twins to be a bad omen, and who will 'disown' any twin babies born within the tribe. It was only with the arrival of Western culture, and most recently French missionaries and charities, that these beliefs and practices have been seriously challenged and many twin babies saved... although even now they are still being rejected by their birth mothers, and need to be raised and cared for in orphanages.

Now, one approach which attempts to resolve the impasse between different cultural beliefs is 'cultural relativism'.

This argues that all cultures are equal, and because of this fact all cultures should be equally respected.

But in my experience, this can only work if:

- You ignore certain 'elements' of what a culture preaches.

- The dominant culture is forced into a subservient role, so that the subservient culture(s) can claim the role of 'victim'.

This is not to say that, in the past, the dominant culture has not carried out real crimes against the subservient cultures. But as soon as any culture claims the role of 'victim' then we are engaged in a cultural 'Karpman Drama Triangle', where the only 3 roles available are *victim, persecutor* and *rescuer*... and these roles can all too easily shift, with the *victim* becoming the *persecutor*, and the *persecutor* the *victim*. This is a game which has been played out in the Middle East for thousands of years.

But the big problem with the whole approach of cultural relativism is you cannot force any culture to respect *all* the beliefs and elements of another culture, just as you cannot make anyone modify or change their own belief system to fall into line with an official dictate of love and peace. Often, to accept something in another culture means that you have to downgrade something in your own culture, and as soon as any people start to feel that their culture is starting to be eroded or dilluted, then they will go on the offensive to save something they consider to be essential to their collective sense of identity and continued survival.

But if any multicultural society is really going to work, then this is something which *everyone* has to do at some point... give up a belief or two in order for everyone to live in harmony and peace with one another. Because it is often only our beliefs which define and divide us.

Although many people reading this chapter will find the idea of killing newborn babies just for the mishap of being born a twin as abhorrent, there are people in Madagascar, who probably love and care for the *rest* of their children, but who also find the idea of killing twins perfectly acceptable... because in their heads twins are evil. They also probably perceive the French missionaries as interfering in their tribal culture, and the orphanges which have rescued the twins as places of great evil which they would burn to the ground given the chance. What a difference a belief makes.

There was a recent B.B.C programme on migrants in the U.K., where a number of migrants were paired with a U.K. citizen for a period of time, at the end of which, the U.K. citizen was asked whether the migrant was a drain on society or a positive contributor.

A Muslim man from war-torn Eritrea was paired with a U.K. citizen, a female Sikh. Although the Muslim male claimed that he was fair minded and tolerant, and had come to the U.K. with his family to escape persecution, it soon became clear that in reality he wasn't prepared to modify his own beliefs or activities in any way to fit in with her approach, or the wider society around him. When she asked him to step inside a Sikh temple for a quick look, or distribute food to the homeless for a Sikh charity, he politely declined, because his faith would not allow him to do so. He said that it was not that he was against the idea of charity and helping his fellow man, just that he preferred to do it through a Muslim organisation.

If one supposedly 'fair minded' human being isn't prepared to budge a little, then how do you ever 'square the circle' between:

- One culture which accepts Gay people and another which actively persecutes them?

- One culture which promotes equal rights for women and another which sees them as second class citizens, refuses to educate them, and even engages in female circumcision (because it is meant to keep the female 'pure')?

- One culture which sees twin babies as evil and is prepared to let them die and another who sees them as just innocent babies who should be loved and protected?

The problem is each human being believes themselves to be 'fair minded'... so long as no one seriously challenges their own belief systems, or expects them to change their ways. But when they are seriously challenged, people will literally go to war to defend their beliefs, and to protect their sense of individual and cultural identity.

To therefore argue that homosexuality is *morally wrong* must be based on the assumption that your version of morality is 100% right which, in the modern age with all its conflicting cultures and morals, is becoming far harder to believe without question. To do so, you literally have to ignore all the other religious and cultures which are around you, stick your fingers in your ears, and shout loudly 'La, la, la... I'm not listening!" Unfortunately, there are people who are prepared to do this, especially when it means that you don't have to think for yourself, because your *special book* contains everything you need to know about life and acceptable human behaviour.

Now, one of the things which you occasionally hear Gay people say is that they wish they could pop into a time machine, and travel back to the time of Ancient Greece and Rome, and live there, because back then Gay sexuality was 'acceptable'.

However, there are a few problems with this view:

• Ancient Greece and Rome was a very male society, and if you were female, then you would have had a much rougher time on the whole. And the elite status was reserved for those individuals who were male, free and rich. If you were poor or a slave, whether male or female, life wasn't very enjoyable at all. Indeed, at one period, women had more freedom in Sparta then in Athens, and in Rome slaves had no rights at all, and their owners could put them to death without any fear of legal repercussions... and the preferred methods of death where sometimes pretty gruesome (in order to set an example to their fellow slaves).

• The freedom between two 'consenting' males was also limited by social and cultural beliefs and conditioning in both Athens and Rome. Normally, in Athens it was limited to an older man 'training' a younger boy, who had to be of the same class, in the role and responsibilities of being a male citizen. In Rome, gay sex was OK, as long as the upper class man never stooped to play the subservient, or female, role. In both societies, two males of the same age and same class would not have been so readily welcomed.

The great tragedy in the life of the Emperor Hadrian (76 to 138) occurred during a tour of Egypt, when his younger Greek male lover, Antinous, drowned while the Imperial party was taking a pleasure cruise down the Nile. To this day, it is generally assumed that Antinous took his own life. However, there is also the possibility that he was murdered. Why? Because while he was still a youth, the relationship between Antinous and Hadrian was 'just about' socially acceptable, but were Antinous to have become a mature man, the same relationship would have been seen as scandalous. Another theory goes that he killed himself to spare Hadrian the shame of this happening. But whatever version of the story is correct, Hadrian never got over his loss.

But the biggest problem with the 'let's pop in a time machine and go back to Ancient Greece or Rome' idea is that... as we have just seen... it wasn't a truly Gay society. In fact, within human history, until recently, there has never been any large, organised society which has been truly supportive of their Gay citizens.[1] Why is that?

Well, let us assume that the figure of 10% of the Ancient Greek population being Gay is roughly correct. Let us also assume that in Athens, during this period, 70% of the male population were engaging in homosexual activity (of some sort), training young boys in how to be men.

Does that mean they were *all* actually Gay? Or were the vast majority Straight Men engaging in homosexual activity for cultural reasons?

Looking at how the numbers stack up, I believe that these were Straight societies which, for some reason, *chose* to engage in homosexual activity... and so were imbalanced, or became imbalanced. We know that at this time the Greeks were a society of warring city states, who were always arguing and jostling for position. There probably was too

---

1   There is an argument to be had over whether modern Western societies are supportive or not, with voices to be raised for and against. However, in many of these modern democracies, legislation has been passed to protect the rights of Gay citizens, which for the sake of this book I believe makes these socities generally supportive, which is unique in human history.

much Yang in this set-up, and we'll be exploring this potential, and its implications, when we come to look at the 10 Energy Polarity types later on in this book.

Why would a male-dominant Straight society want to do this? Well, contrary to anything which you may hear from the Pentagon, male soliders who have sex with one another can be a very good thing from a military point of view, because there is a lot of Yang and male aggression generated, which the army can focus on the enemy.

If you have a bond with your fellow soliders, then often you will fight to the death, which is something that happened with the Corinthian *Band of Brothers*, also known as *The Sacred Band of Thebes* (who were all made up of 150 pairs of male lovers) who did indeed fight to the death when they fought their last battle against Philip II of Macedon (382 to 336 B.C.), with his young son Alexander the Great (356 to 323 B.C.), in 338 B.C at the Battle of Chaeronea. They stood their ground and fought on, even though the rest of their army had deserted the battlefield.[2] On viewing the corpses, Philip II is meant to have said, 'Perish any man who suspects that these men either did or suffered anything unseemly.' The Spartans used the same approach with their soldiers, which helped to create a powerful and cohesive fighting force.

Now, in our culture, all of this has been watered down by 2000 years of Christianity, so that now any such behaviour between men sounds totally alien and weird. Homosexuals are meant to be weak, not individuals who will fight on long after their fellow Straight warriors have deserted the battlefield. But remember, this is because we live in a different time and culture.

---

2   Remember, Alexander also had a male lover, called Hephaestion (356 to 324 B.C), who was probably the true love of his life, but who could never be publically acknowledged because of the need for the King to marry a Queen and produce a legitimate heir to the throne. Bascially, true love was frustrated by power politics and tradition.

But it did once happen. The psychologist Paul Ekman in his book *Emotions Revealed* also writes about a tribal society in Papua New Guinea called the Anga where homosexuality amongst the men was dominant, and this created a very aggressive society, where mature men would prey upon young boys. Instead of creating a weak and efiminate society, such behvaiour appears to create a more aggressive and hostile society, and the Anga were noted for their hostile and aggressive behavior towards neighbouring tribes and outsiders.

But once again, I would argue that this is Straight men engaging in sexual acts, which as we shall see when we discuss the Energy Polarity Types, can lead to all kinds of problems.

Modern psychologists say that newborn babies are only programmed with two natural fears, which are the *fear of loud noises* and the *fear of falling*. Every other fear they acquire from other people, from the culture around them.

And the same appears to be true for much of our moral codes... no matter how uncomfortable this makes us feel. Very little is underwritten by divine or natural law. This is why many religions have complex laws and rules with regards to human behaviour and sin. OK, we do need laws and rules to help human beings co-exist... but through placing them within a spiritual context, through making it look like they came direct from God... it makes it look as if God cares, is taking an interest, and will punish those who break his / her divine laws.

However, the reality is that much of our moral codes and laws arose from the prejudice of a single human, or group of human beings, long, long ago, and so are not underwritten by any divine or natural force. And what is morality anyway. It's a map to help guide and support a human being, from cradle to grave, a map to help them control their behaviour and levels of anxiety, a map to help them navigate their way through life, and fit in with the fellow members of their tribe or society. Because if you think, feel and behave like everyone else there is less chance of your being treated as an 'outsider'. Morality is often just another name for social camouflage.

When your mind, your emotions, your body, and your sexuality cannot fit in with the morality of those around you... that's when you are in real trouble. Unless you can move and hook-up with a more evolved and enlightened tribe. This is why Straight morality makes pariahs of Gay people, because they don't behave as the moral code, dicated by Straight people, demands they should.

That does not mean any Straight moral code is either divinely right and just. It just means it is another set of rules drawn up by a set of human beings... and we all know how fallible human beings can be... especially when they lived 2,000 plus years ago, and their whole life experience was limited to wondering around the rocky wastes of the Sinai desert peninsula for 40 years, desperately trying to find the exit sign to the promise land.

C6. Spirituality & the Whole Gay Thing:

Now in this chapter we *could* explore the question of homosexuality in relation to 'conventional' spirituality. Indeed, we *could* take the time to explore questions such as:

• Is the Dalai Lama right in his traditional Buddhist view on homosexuality?

• Was the 19th Century Indian mystic Ramakrishna sympathetic to Gay people?

• Was the 20th Century mystic Osho *for* or *against* homosexuality?

• Is that 'nice' Pope Francis ever likely to come out in favour of homosexuality?

We could… … But we're not going to... Why?

Because exploring Straight spiritual traditions, looking for some shred of evidence in favour of Gay spirituality, is rather like sifting though the sand grains on a beach hoping to find one grain of rice. Enough has been written about these topics by others, and personally, I don't want to spend time here adding to these debates. I believe these kind of debates to be 'dead ends', because they don't go anywhere interesting, and above all they don't lead to a tangible and workable path for Gay spirituality.

Instead, I would rather spend time exploring the only spiritual tradition which I know of which has seriously and consistently 'incorporated' Gay people into its practices and beliefs. This is the Shamanic tradition.

The Shamanic tradition is the most ancient spiritual tradition on the planet, probably around 40,000 years old, stretching back into the hunter-gatherer origins of the human race. In fact, it is probably far older than that, but it is hard to find the hard archaeological evidence to support an earlier date. Suffice to say, it is the oldest spiritual tradition on the planet.

Taoism and Tantra certainly grew out of the Shamanic traditions in their parts of the world, and it is probably the origin of many other established spiritual traditions (although you won't ever get them to admit this). Tibetan Buddhism was / is heavily influenced by its own native shamanic tradition, which was known as Bön... although as Peter Kingsley points out in his book A *Story Waiting to Pierce You*, Tibetan Buddhists actively and violently persecuted the Bön tradition for many centuries, all with the sanction and quiet blessing of the first Dalai Lamas. They even persuaded the Mongol hordes to do their bloody work for them, and thousands of Bön were killed. After the massacres, Tibetan Buddhism was free to incorporate Bön concepts and practices into their own tradition without anyone left to accuse them of plagiarism (so much for the Dalai Lamas being direct incarnations of the Buddha of Compassion).

It is true that Shamanic traditions are varied and different throughout the world, but they do share many common themes, beliefs and practices, which may stretch back to a common cultural origin, located somewhere in the Middle East or Africa.

Let's start by going back say 15,000 or 20,000 years... long before the first agricultural revolution (when people realised they could grow their own food and so live in one place all year round).

How was human culture structured back then? Well, it was a hunter-gatherer culture, made up of small tribes, travelling around, following the seasons and herds, going where the food was. Let's say that there are 70 people in one such nomadic tribe, travelling across the plains, following the herds. For practical reasons, this tribe could not support a population which was too large, and so everyone in the tribe knew everyone else. It was a very close knit affair. To avoid the dangers of interbreeding, they probably met-up with other tribes, from time to time, to inter-marry perhaps. But on the whole, tribes probably kept much to themselves for long periods of time.

Now, if we apply the modern rule that 10% of the population is Gay... and there is no reason to believe that the female womb behaved any differently back then than now... then that would mean that 7 people in our 70 strong tribe had a homosexual orientation.

How would the rest of the tribe have behaved towards these 7 Gay individuals in their midst? Well, if someone does something within any tribe which is 'beyond the pale', then they will probably be either killed or ostracised, kicked out to die on their own without the protection of the tribe... and the chances of their being accepted into another tribe was very slim to non-existent. So it is *possible* that these Gay people could have been killed, or kicked out of their tribe, when their secret became 'known', which is what happens in many countries and cultures in our modern age.

But to be honest... that just doesn't make sense, because it would mean that, on a regular basis, the tribe would be losing 10% of its man / woman power, and in a hostile world each tribe *would need all the people it could get*.

The tribe would need these people to help hunt, to gather fruit, to help protect it... So to me, it just doesn't make sense for any tribe to lose useful hands, either through killing or expelling them without good cause.

A hunter-gatherer tribe cannot allow itself to get too big, or else it has too many mouths to feed. But conversely, a tribe cannot afford to get too small, or else it runs the risk of becoming unviable. Also, in such small human groups, tribal and family bonds are likely to be very strong, and will work to keep Gay people within the tribe if at all possible. You wouldn't be persecuting and evicting an 'unknown' person, you would be ostracising your brother or sister, your cousin, or your close friend, and so they would need to have done something really, really bad for you to turn against them.

Overall, 20,000 year ago, I believe it was more beneficial for the tribe to develop ideas, beliefs, and a culture which allowed these Gay people to stay within the tribe, and continue to make a positive contribution to the group. Killing or ostracising them would have been too much of a waste of resources. And indeed, this is what we find in many shamanic cultures and traditions. Gay people were *accepted* and given a *role*.

If we consider what Holger Kalweit writes in his book *Dreamtime & Inner Space: The World of the Shaman*:

> *In some tribal communities the acquisition of power and initiation as a shaman is accompanied by a change of sex. Among the Siberian Chuckchee there are womanlike men and menlike women, that is to say women who have changed into men, and vice versa. They will even marry a member of the same sex, and if a manlike woman wants to have children, she enters into an "exchange marriage," into which the desired child is born... not every sexual transient becomes a shaman, but transients are referred to by a special name: the soft womanly man is known as an Anasik and his counterpart, the mannish woman, as an Uktesik.*[1]

In the modern age, Gay men and women, who are in partnership, are finding ways to have children and so establish families... usually with the help of Straight / Gay men and women who are happy to provide them with sperm or wombs. To some in the popular press this is an abomination, shouldn't be allowed, and will bring about the end of civilisation. However, as Kalweit points out, this kind of thing has probably been going on for *millennia* in shamanic cultures around

1   Holger Kalweit, pages 180 to 181.

the world, and humanity seems to have survived OK up to now.

In his book, Kalweit points out that:

• There were various graduations of sexual transformation within the tribes, and so an individual could choose, or be guided by spirit, to adopt that level which best suited their own inner nature. Not all sexual transients walked down the shamanic path, and the tribe still found a place for them within the community.

• As shamans, such sexual transients were believed to have a heightened sensitivity for their environment, for their own energy and for the energy of other people. Although the subject of some scorn, these shamans were even more feared and respected than the ordinary heterosexual shamans.

• Sexually abnormal shamans or medicine men are found in many other cultures around the world.

Unfortunately, Kalweit also points out that these customs have now largely died out in many North American tribes, due to the influence of Western culture and Christianity.

On the website www.examiner.com, Richard Thornton also writes about the position of Gay people within different Native American cultures:

Cherokees also had a tolerant attitude toward sexual manifestation. Any Cherokees today expressing homophobic attitudes are not within the realm of Cherokee tradition. The Cherokee concept of homosexuality can be translated in English as "two spirited." Cherokees believed that having attraction to both men and women was normal, although not characteristic of all Cherokees. It is quite possible that Cherokee gay men functioned as paramedics like those of the Arawak Alecmanis. It was common for Cherokee lesbians to fight in battle. They would shoot arrows and later, fire muskets, in support of ground assaults.[2]

He also points out that at this time the Native American tribes really were not obsessed with the different expressions of human sexuality, as the European explorerers were.

Now, we have to remember that this is a picture drawn from anthropological research at the start of the 20th Century, and many of these tribal practices no longer exist, having been washed away through over-exposure to Western culture and Christian missionaries. As Thornton writes, any Cherokees today expressing homophobic views are not practising their own traditions of tolerance and inclusion, but those of the dominant Western culture. So there is strong evidence that, before this, within Shamanic cultures, probably stretching back thousands of years:

• Gay individuals were able to live productive lives within their tribes / cultures, prospered within the group, and were accepted to a lesser or greater degree.

• Some of these individuals were valued for their psychic / spiritual talents and gifts, and were put to work as healers and shamans for the tribe. Their unique energy make-up seems to have given them access to, as Kalweit puts it, 'a heightened sensitivity for their environment, themselves, and their inner strengths and energies'.

• There is a hint that there were others who did not become 'soft men' or 'hard women', but who happily married the soft men and hard women, and were then able to continue to live within their tribe as normal Straight men and women. This would imply that both effeminate and masculine Gay men and women were

2   http://www.examiner.com/article/native-americans-and-sexuality

all given active roles within the tribe. Or that some Straight men / women were happy to have a soft man / hard woman as their 'life partner'. Whatever is true… sexual roles and preferences were much more fluid and flexible back then.

• Although I didn't know this at the time when I was developing this theory, Native American cultures traditionally referred to Gay people as being 'two-spirited', as having the spirit of a man and the spirit of a woman, and so they were seen as being more spiritually gifted than the typical masculine man or feminine woman. Therefore, within Native American cultures, rather than persecuting these Gay people, the tribe looked to them to become leaders and shamans. Very soon we will see that the title of 'two-spirited' is very apt indeed.

Now, if we also go on to assume (and will be exploring this in more detail soon) that from a spiritual perspective, Gay people have certain advantages in the inner world over their Straight counterparts, then there is no surprise in the fact that many Gay people often became shamans themselves.

Through transforming them into Shamans, soft or otherwise, their tribe was able to benefit from their psychic / spiritual gifts, and these individuals were given valued social roles within their communities as 'guides' and 'healers'. So at this time in human history… the practicalities of survival probably over-ruled intolerance and prejudice. For around 30,000 years, it was OK to be Gay.

Now, let's fast forwards in time to the Agricultural revolution, which occurred around 10,000 B.C. People started to settle down in favourable locations, usually along large rivers such as the Nile or Euphrates, coming together to form city-states or kingdoms, planted crops which led to a surplus of food, the population started to grow… and human civilisation started to create 'support roles' that were not directly related to the growing or gathering of food.

These new roles include that of the *King* and the *Priest*. Basically, these are people with time on their hands, people with something to 'prove'. Because if you are someone who is at the top of your city's food chain, and you are not doing anything yourself to grow the food you eat, then you need to have a very good reason for doing what you do. Your contribution to the community has to be so great that it justifies others growing your food for you. So we are into the business of 'job justification'.

For example:

> *"I am a priest, I don't have time to grow my own food, but you should keep feeding me because I make a valuable contribution to our culture in the following way... I have a direct link to the Gods, I can read the scriptures and holy books, which contain the rules which we all need to follow. In fact, no one else can speak to the Gods except through me. I am special, so you need to keep feeding me."*

OK, I might be being a bit cynical here... but I bet there was an element of that going on back then. To be honest, this is the same argument which priests have been using, right down to the present day, to justify their position within human society. 'You can't speak directly to God, but I can, because I am special... so respect and feed me!'

Unfortunately, for our discussion, during this period I believe the role of Gay people started to change and diminish... and the persecution started. In a city state of 10,000 people, if you suddenly lost 1,000 heads, it might be an inconvenience for a year or two, but the city would survive in the long-term. And in a population of 10,000 people you can't expect to know everyone, and so the old tribal bounds and loyalties start to break down. Your loyalty is to your immediate family, the King and the Priest... not to some unknown stranger on the other side of the city who has suddenly been accused of 'unnatural practices'.

So, because of population growth, Gay people became less important to keep within society because there were enough Straight people around to grow and gather the food from the fields. The King / Priests had so many Straight hands that they didn't need to keep the Gay people around to help with the work. In fact, Gay people became far more useful to the Priests as an enemy, as a scapegoat, as a wrong-doer, someone to point the figure at and blame when things weren't going too well for the city-state. It suddenly became much easier, and more useful, to exclude and persecute them.

During this period of human history, the Priests were able to justify their position by showing that they were protecting the people / city state against evil and unnatural practices, which if left unchecked would bring down the wrath of God on the whole population (i.e. the whole Sodom and Gomorrah scenario). And whenever you create rules, then you also automatically create people who are breaking those rules, and so who need to be 'punished'... and so the Priests set about writing down God's holy rule book, including things like:

> • *Leviticus 18: 'You shall not lie with a male as with a woman; it is an abomination.'*

> • *Leviticus 20 'If a man lies with a male as with a woman, both of them have committed an abomination; they shall surely be put to death; their blood is upon them.'*

Is it any wonder then that Gays became the perfect target?

Now as we shall see in later chapters, unfortunately the polarity works against Gay people in these group situations (especially when a Gay Man has to inter-act with an insecure Straight Alpha male). This is why I believe, slowly over time, the positive role of Gay people in shamanic cultures was lost, and they were edged out of the Straight religions which came next. Because the Straight Kings and Priests didn't need Gay people, didn't value them, and got more mileage out of them being scapegoats and wrong doers.

Plus, if Gay people did have certain advantages when it comes to plugging into the inner world, Straight Priests may have also been envious of this, and so wanted to deny them any kind of psychic or spiritual role in their communities. As far as the priests were concerned, they had the only monopoly of speaking directly to God... and wanted to root out and destroy any competition.

The same thing happened when Christianity took over the Western world. The wise women, who were a challenge and threat to the male Christian clergy, were demonised and turned into 'witches', who were all supposedly in league with the Devil, and were eventually burnt at the stake. Many of these women were probably only the local midwife or herbalist, and so killing them inflicted untold harm on their communities... but secured the position of the local Catholic priest.

So, when we put things into this historical context, is it any wonder that our current religions, which have been passed down to us from these far distant times, are so violently anti-Gay? But if we look deeper into pre-history, back to the oldest spiritual tradition on the planet, to shamanism, we discover a completely different story entirely.

Indeed, as we shall see, and as Holger Kalweit suggests, compared to the Straights, Gay people may just be plugged into a superfast broadband connection to the spirit world... And where in the Straight spiritual texts and literature have you ever read someone say that before?

C7. Historical Context - A Crazy Thought Experiement:

Albert Einstein made many of his important discoveries through what he called 'thought experiments'. A thought experiment is where, instead of conducting an experiment within a physical laboratory, the experiment is conducted entirely within the scientist's own mind, or on paper.

Thought experiments can be useful because they help a scientist think outside of the 'box' and also draw upon their intuitive mind, although, thought experiments still require a real-world experiment to be conducted at a later date to prove that the initial conclusions of the thought experiment are indeed correct. Einstein's most famous thought experiment was when he imagined what would happen if he were to ride upon a beam of light, travelling at the speed of light. That thought experiment led to his discovery of *The Theory of Relativity*, and it literally re-wrote our understanding of how the universe works.

I now propose to also conduct a 'thought experiment' of my own, to help us understand how Gay Tantra may possibly have developed over the period of human history... Or how it may have come off the rails... or never even got off the ground. So... Let us imagine a scene, 3,000 to 4,000 years ago, just on the edge of recorded human history.

This scene takes place in Northern India... or China... or possibly Egypt. Somewhere where the human race has established a stable and flourishing civilisation, where people are able to live relatively safe, secure and productive lives, and pass down their knowledge and skills from generation to generation. It takes place in a location which is isolated from the main human population centres of the time, perhaps deep in the mountains, or maybe out in the desert.

Let us imagine, that in this place, a small group of male and female

Tantric practitioners, of different ages and experiences, have gathered together to deepen their spiritual / energy practices, pairing up, man with woman, woman with man. Because their beliefs and practices are not shared by the rest of their culture, which potentially opens them up to ridicule or persecution, they have gathered in this remote area, where they will not easily be found or disturbed.

They are led by an ancient man and woman, Tantric masters, who are located in the exact centre of their group. Here, in the wilderness, they have gathered for the past month, to learn, to practice, to share, to deepen their spiritual energies... and they have been making steady progress, until...

In the middle of their camp, a young man suddenly appears. He is youthful, strong, handsome, perhaps 21 years of age. He has a charismatic, dynamic presence... and must have been guided by the Gods, otherwise how could he have found their group in the middle of this vast wilderness, which is miles from the nearest human habitation.

He gracefully weaves his way through the circle of students, and walks straight up to the two Masters, in the centre. He bows reverently, and humbly asks to be admitted into their select group. He wishes to learn about the art and science of Tantra.

He presents them with a letter from a Great Spiritual Master, who lives far to the South, but who is much revered throughout the land. This Master writes that this young man is a genuine and talented spiritual aspirant. He writes that this young man is worthy of serious consideration as a potential candidate for admission to their select group.

So... he is youthful, strong, cultured and healthy... He has travelled a long way, overcome many obstacles to reach them... He must have been guided by the Gods to find them... And he is highly recommended by another genuine and well-respected spiritual master. Finding a spiritual man is rare at the best of times (just ask any group of New Age women), but one who is also educated, strong and healthy? He ticks *all* the boxes.

But just when the two Masters are about to announce that they formally accept him into their group as a Novice / Apprentice...The young man says:

> "Actually, I am only sexually attracted to other men... I hope that won't be a problem?"

... There is a hushed silence throughout the group. This has never happened before.

In fact, some members of the group have *never* even considered the possibility that two members of the same sex could be attracted to each other 'in that way'. Surely, it's against the will of the Gods! So the group waits to see how their Masters will react.

What happens next? Do they:

- Burn him alive?

- Stone him to death?

- Throw him out, roughed up a little but still alive?

- Say 'Sorry, there is nothing we can do to help', and politely send him on his way?

- Say 'No problem, welcome to our group!' and introduce him to Gary?

Let's assume that these two Masters really are spiritually enlightened, that they have developed beyond their crude cultural conditioning, and have achieved a state of compassion towards all living beings...

so we can strike the first three options from the list. Which leaves them with the two remaining options, either polite rejection, or acceptance.

The male and female Tantric Masters look at each other. After decades of spiritual work together, they are so in tune that they know instantly what their partner is thinking without having to say a word. You see, their problem is that if they accept him into their group:

• Who could possibly work with him, as no one else in the group shares his particular 'attractions', and to make one of the male members work with him would be 'wrong' for that individual (i.e. there is no Gary).

• How will sexual energy flow between two men in a spiritual context? There is nothing in their experience, or the ancient texts written by a long tradition of heterosexual masters, to help them answer that question, and to completely understand it, they would have to devote their consciousness to this question, and this would take their time and attention away from rest of the group. This would mean 50 students would suffer for the sake of one.

After some telepathic consultation, consideration and deliberation, they decide... It's not just worth it. With compassion in their voice, they reply:

"We are sorry, there is nothing we can do... you must leave."

The young man rises, dejectedly, and slowly turns to leave.

(If I were him, after such a long journey, at this point I'd probably be muttering 'Thanks a bunch' under my breath. But he is a better man than I, and so says nothing as he quietly leaves.)

But fortunately for him, the Great Female Spirit who has had a hand in getting him here, isn't one to give up without a fight, and so gives a helpful nudge in the right direction at this vital moment...

Just as the young man is about to leave their camp forever, the female Tantric master comes after him and says...

> "Although we cannot help you, there may be a spiritual path that you could walk. But you will need to find it for yourself, and you will need a partner, such as yourself, who can walk it with you... Good luck."

With those final words of encouragement, the young man turns, leaves their camp, instilled with a new sense of hope, and sets out on a quest to find a compatible partner, a soul mate, who can help him to carve out this new Gay Tantric path (only he wouldn't have used the word 'gay', obviously, he would have called it something else).

The young man sets off, once again, on his noble quest...but this time with a totally different objective.

Now, remember, we're talking 3,000 to 4,000 years ago. There were no internet dating sites, no mass transportation systems, so he would have to travel from city to city, town to town, village to village, 'quietly' searching for someone like himself, not drawing too much attention, seeking someone who was attracted to other men, someone who was being called home by spirit, someone who was attracted to him and his true 'calling'... someone who was aware of who and what he was, accepted it, and was prepared to take the risk when the opportunity appeared.

Not easy. Not now, even with all our technical perks, and definitely not then. Although it is set in Edwardian England, and not Ancient Mesopotamia, China or Egypt, the movie *Maurice*, based on the novel by E.M. Forster, can give you some idea of the difficulties and problems of two gay men finding each other, and establishing a real relationship, within an 'unsupportive' culture... that's if you don't already know that from first-hand experience.

Let's assume it took him 20 years to achieve this, which means at the age of 41 years he finds a suitable partner, a Gay Tantric soul mate. But the problem then is that time is running out for them, life expectancy during this period was probably 30 to 50 years for men (if they were lucky and avoided wars, plague, famine and persecution). So, if they are lucky, our two Gay Tantric practitioners have around 10 years in which to work together and discover a spiritual path which supports their uniqueness... a spiritual path which is completely new.

Because we have to remember that there will be nothing much in the established teachings and literature of the time to help them in their search (and books were also rare and priceless commodities back then, and most wisdom was transmitted verbally). Anything they do find in the religious teachings relating to homosexuality will probably be extremely 'negative', and so they would need to ignore and overcome any condemnation and prejudice if they were going to succeed. They are starting afresh... completely.

But, once again, let's assume that they were successful, that the Great Mother smiled upon them, gave them a few intuitive pointers, and they discovered a viable / workable Gay Tantric path, one which can return a Gay individual or couple to their spiritual 'home'. Unfortunately, they now encounter a final problem. After travelling so far, and overcoming so much... Who are they going to pass their knowledge on to?

During all periods of human history... to create a viable spiritual tradition you need reliable, dedicated students to pass your knowledge on to, who will then pass this knowledge on to their students, who will then pass it on to their students... etc... etc... (you get the picture). And it's not just a question of passing down knowledge... Any book can do that... It's really a question of passing down *spiritual wisdom*. This means that at least one individual in each generation has to take the knowledge being passed down, work with it, and successfully achieve 'enlightenment'… so when they speak to the next generation, the words are alive with the force of their spiritual realisation (i.e. been there, done that, got the spiritual t-shirt).

Although we must always remember that the concept of 'enlightenment' means different things to different spiritual traditions. For some it is the 'destination', for others it is a stopover on a much longer journey. If that happens then the tradition remains 'alive'.

However, when that stops, when there is no 'brave' individual within the next generation… the tradition dies, it becomes a *dead tradition*… a tradition that is based on priests repeating dry words from sacred books, words which no longer carry the power to *change* and *transform*.

If this is a problem for most, indeed all heterosexual spiritual traditions across time… and many have died out as the calibre of their students declined… you can almost guarantee that, back then, it would be a downright impossibility for a fledgling spiritual homosexual tradition to gather together enough students to ensure the continuation of the tradition within a single generation. And even if you managed to find two suitable and compatible students to form a tradition which could keep the tradition alive, you would need to keep repeating it for generation after generation after generation… and all in secret, to avoid persecution.

So at this point in our 'thought experiment' there is a real danger that the knowledge and practices of Gay Tantra, hard won by these two individuals, will be lost.

A religion also survives through breeding the next generation, and then indoctrinating them at an early age into following the 'established' religious doctrine. However, our two Gay Masters don't have that option here. One of the quirks of the universe is that, if a Gay man and a Gay woman do have a baby together, the likelihood will be that the baby *won't be homosexual.*

But there is another option they could try to continue their new tradition, communication through the written word. It's not ideal, because the written word can be misinterpreted, which is why spiritual masters have always preferred working within an oral tradition, or one where the living master can correctly explain first-hand the ancient texts for the benefit of their students. But our two Gay Tantric masters don't have that luxury, so with time running out, they decide to write down all their hard-won knowledge, this new path they have discovered, on several duplicate papyrus texts, which are safely deposited in different places across the land. Their hope is that at least one of these texts will be found by the right person, and like a seed finding the right soil, it will take root and grow again.

Then, finally, they die... together, in each other's arms... (OK, let's give them a nice, romantic passing, I think they've earned it). After their death, the ancient texts remain hidden for hundreds of years. In that time:

• One of the texts is accidentally destroyed when the monastery is burnt to the ground by a novice monk trying to cook sausages (which he shouldn't have been doing because sausages are forbidden in his particular spiritual tradition).

• Another text is used by mice to build their nest, and so is lost.

• Another text, buried, rots away in damp earth when a river changes its course over time, and so is lost.

• Another text is buried deep under a landslide, caused by an earthquake, and so is lost.

• And the final text is burnt by a religious fanatic, who found it, read it, and destroyed it as being 'blasphemous'... (and a lot of ancient knowledge has been lost this way, especially when spiritual 'fashions' change).

And so, their hard won knowledge and discoveries becomes slowly lost as the centuries pass...

But, during human history, this has happened time and time again. When the Great Library of Alexandria burnt down, it probably set human history civilisation back hundreds of years. Another set-back was when the Romans raided the island of Corfu, which was once a great centre of knowledge and learning in the Mediterranean. Because the Romans needed its treasure house of gold to fund another one of their wars, they destroyed its centres of learning in the process, which never recovered. The Romans didn't really do 'learning', unless it led to better rhetoric, trade, farming or siege engines.

The First Chinese Emperor ordered all books in the Empire to be burnt, and their knowledge erased, and anyone who defied this Imperial decree was buried alive with their books (Pol Pot did a similar thing in Cambodia in the 1970s which his attempt to reset everything to 'Year 0'). And the mother of the Byzantine Emperor Justinian built up a great library of spiritual texts from different Mediterranean civilisations, which was then destroyed after her death, because it wasn't considered to be 'Christian'.

In our 21st Century Western fortress, we tend to assume, once gained, knowledge is *forever*. But, unfortunately, history shows that knowledge can be easily lost if circumstances change. And as I write, there are legions of fundamentalists out there, of all persuasions, who are hell bent on destroying all knowledge which doesn't agree with their black and white version of the 'truth'. But knowledge which is lost can also be *re-discovered*, which is what the Italian Renaissance was all about, and this is a much more encouraging thought altogether (to quote Gandalf the Grey)... **Although it may take several centuries, be a painful process, and several Giordano Brunos will likely be burnt at the stake along the way for believing in and preaching the wrong thing.**

So, this brings our 'thought experiment' to an end. What have we learnt?

Well, what I would say we have learnt is that, in pre-history and early human history, if the development of Gay Tantra was indeed possible, the chances of it developing and taking root were very, very slim. It would have required sufficient numbers of spiritually inclined Gay people to come together, generation after generation, to not only discover Gay Tantra, but to also pass it on successfully to others, without being persecuted or destroyed, and their knowledge lost. But for most of recorded history, the social and cultural conditions simply did not exist to allow that to happen.

In our thought experiment, our hero was a Gay Man. If we change them into a Gay heroine then, historically, the chips were stacked up even more against the possibility of Gay Tantra developing. Because women, whatever their sexual orientation, have often had a more restricted life in many cultures, and so would have had less opportunity to travel and develop an enquiring mind and knowledge base. They suffered greater repression then men, and in many countries, they still do. For example, check out the life and death of Hypatia, a female philosopher at the University of Alexandria (370 to 415 A.D.) who was killed horrifically by a crowd of Christian fanatics because she was trying to embrace and expand the field of human knowledge.

It's only **now**, in the last 20 to 30 years, that the social and cultural conditions have arisen, in a limited number of liberal Western countries, which could potentially support the development of Gay Tantra. But there is no guarantee that those conditions will continue on into the future. For **now**, for those spiritually inclined Gay individuals born into supportive countries and cultures, the possibility is there. So perhaps we should run the ball with it while we can, for as long as we can.

Another thing which I believe is true, and can be shown through this thought experiment, is that Gay Tantra is not an offshoot of Straight Tantra. Straight Tantra practitioners would *never* develop Gay Tantra... why would they, there is no point. It would be like writing a book in French for an audience of German readers.

Straight Tantra was created by heterosexuals for heterosexuals, and there is nothing wrong with this. But if Gay Tantra does exist... and we'll explore that question next... it is something which needs to be created by Gay people for Gay people.

Indeed, there must actually be two streams within Gay Tantra, one for Gay men and one for Gay women, which respects and supports their energetic differences. Also Gay Tantra isn't Straight Tantra with a few minor modifications. It is fundamentally a different beast entirely, and needs to be built from the bottom up (please forgive the double meaning there).

Let me explain further about why this has to be so. The spiritual master, Hazrat Inayat Khan, who brought Sufism to the West from India in the early 20th Century, used to say that the universal source of knowledge was a bit like a warehouse filled to the roof which different objects, artwork, scientific equipment and discoveries, and literary texts... all waiting to be discovered. But the warehouse itself is completely dark... no light whatsoever... you have to bring your own light (and this light is based on your level of consciousness). So, to find whatever you want, you had to bring your own torch.

Let's imagine that four men go into this dark warehouse, each armed with a small, hand-held torch. One man is a painter, another man is a scientist, another is a writer, and the last man is a musician. What do they find as they move around this warehouse, stuffed to roof with all the potential discoveries of human civilisation?

Well...

- The painter finds a painting by Rembrandt, another by Picasso, and another by Monet.

- The scientist finds an electron microscope, a revolutionary overlooked invention by Nikolai Tesla, and the large hadron collider (it's a big warehouse).

- The writer finds an original portfolio of Shakespeare's plays, a first edition of Mark Twain, and a complete edition of the plays of George Bernard Shaw.

- The musician finds a violin by Stradivarius, a piano used by Chopin, and a guitar used by Jimmy Hendrix.

So... what is the point of this story? Well, according to Hazrat Inayat Khan, we only pull out of this 'warehouse of all knowledge' that which interests us, that which we are attracted to, that which we are inspired by.

The warehouse is stuffed full of musical instruments, or literary texts, but the scientists doesn't see them, they're invisible to him, because his consciousness is only focused on scientific pursuits (and even that can be broken down into sub-categories – physics, chemistry, biology...) Likewise, the musician walks past all the scientific equipment, without noticing them, because his awareness is totally focused on all the musical instruments he can see around him. (OK, I am sure there are a few scientists out there shouting 'But I play the piano as well, I'm a well-rounded individual!' And likewise, I am sure there are a few indignant musicians saying 'But I studied mathematics at college!') Hopefully you get the point I am trying to make here.

When we apply this 'principle of consciousness' to the subject of Tantra, we can see that, because the Tantric masters of the past were heterosexuals, they only pulled out from the 'warehouse of all knowledge' that which was beneficial for them and their students, their tradition. They pulled out *Straight Tantra*.

Now... if the Universe is indeed compassionate, and not some big cosmic joke against the Gays... then I believe if Gay people, who are sincere and spiritually inclined, go into this transcendental warehouse, then they should and will find the knowledge, understanding and techniques which are meant for them. For how can a compassionate universe **not** supply this knowledge to them if they sincerely ask? Strangely, this is a belief I was born with, and the whole of this work is 'rooted', has been 'fuelled', by this belief.

But only Gay people can go into the warehouse on their own behalf. Only Gay people can ask for the information which applies to them. Only Gay people can develop *Gay Tantra*.

Gay people can look to other spiritual traditions for insight and inspiration. But the answers they/we seek about Gay spiritual sexuality will not be found 'entirely' in traditions developed by heterosexuals.

We can't expect Straight people to solve our spiritual problems for us. Gay Tantra needs to be created by Gay people for Gay people (with help from a loving, compassionate, interested universe). And there has never been a better time for that to happen then now.

Here endeth the lesson...

... Let's move on to the next chapter in our story.

PART TWO

Well, if it's so deep you don't think that you can speak about it,
Just remember to reach out and touch the past and the future.
Well, if it's so deep you don't think you can speak about it,
Don't ever think that you can't change the past and the future.
You might not, not think so now,
But just you wait and see--someone will come to help you.

Kate Bush
Love & Anger

C8.Energy Dynamics & Polarity:

In his book *The Tao of Health, Sex & Longevity*, Daniel Reid writes that from a Taoist medical perspective, homosexual relations between women are considered to be harmless, whereas sexual relations between men are considered to be dangerous and harmful to their health and wellbeing. This is because women are perceived as an expression of Yin, and Yin is not an aggressive force, but passive and yielding. In contrast, men are an expression of Yang, and Yang is perceived as an aggressive and dominating force. When two male energies meet they will automatically come into conflict, without the presence of Yin to bring balance and harmony.

Now we're getting to the Big Question at the heart of Gay Tantra. To be honest, if we can't crack this one wide open, then we might as well give up. Because this is the one which is laid against Gay people, time and again, by the Straight Tantra crowd:

> *We love you Gay people, we love hanging out with you, you're funny, you have a unique perspective on life, honest... but your energy polarity is all 'wrong'... so there is nothing we can do for you (sorry)!*

I once met a Gay guy, who had inadvertently booked himself on to a Tantra course for men. Of course... all the men on the course were straight, and that was the attitude the course leader took with him (and I don't think he ever got a refund either).

This is why this book is called *Gay Polarity Tantra*. Because the whole question of whether Gay people can use sexual energy for personal and spiritual development / meditation centres around this whole question of 'polarity'.

As you can see from Daniel Reid's quote above, this is especially true for Gay men. Within Chinese energy medicine, the view is that Gay women aren't doing themselves any harm, so just let them keep doing it if it makes them happy... but for Gay men it is completely different... stop them, they're actually *harming* themselves!

Now, earlier in this book, I stated that I don't believe the answer (if there is one) to this issue of polarity can be found in Straight Tantra. Because in Straight Tantra a man, whether gay or straight, is *usually* defined as being 100% Yang / Solar, and a woman is defined as being 100% Yin / Lunar... and each one uses their partner's energy to balance out their own energy imbalance. There is no middle ground. It's 'either / or'.

OK, there is Single Cultivation, but even here the male is seen as being predominantly Yang, and the woman as predominantly Yin, so internally there isn't enough of the opposing polarity to help bring that individual's energy into a state of balance. So Single Cultivation is often considered to be a more difficult path to take.

There are writers who, like Daniel Reid, believe that Gay Tantra is *impossible* because the couple cannot draw on / in the opposite polarity to achieve balance. If a Gay couple engage in sexual intercourse they are only amplifying their predominant polarity, which is OK for Gay women, dangerous for Gay men. Although, there is an argument that the danger for Gay women is that, with all the extra Yin, their energies can become too 'stagnant', which can also lead to health and psychological issues as well.

However, there are writers, such as Mantak Chia, who suggest that Gay people could draw upon sources of Yin and Yang 'external' to themselves to help them achieve a balance point between Yin & Yang. If they could do that, then it might be possible to establish a Gay Tantra that could 'work'.

A Gay male couple would need to find an external source of Yin, and a Gay female couple would have to find an external source of Yang, to help them balance out their own naturally occurring internal 'imbalance'. The same would also be true for someone practising Single Cultivation. External sources of Yin include the Earth and Moon, while external sources of Yang include the Sun, and energy techniques exist to help people draw these energies into themselves. However, these sources of Yin and Yang are 'external' and not 'internal'.

So according to this model, Gay men and women have to make *extra effort*, compared to their Straight compatriots, just to reach the *same level*. It would be a like competing in a race where a Gay and Straight couple are running on the same track, but the Gay couple have to run for a longer distance just to reach the same finishing line.

Because the current literature stresses that there is no internal source of Yin within Gay men, nor an internal source of Yang within Gay women, which is sufficient enough to balance and stabilize the opposing polarity for an individual or couple.

According to the current Straight Tantra literature, these are the only two possibilities.

- No such thing as Gay Tantra.

- Gay Tantra where the couple has to work harder than the Straight Couple.

End of story. Life's not fair (get used to it).

I don't believe that is correct... and my direct 'energy' experience is also that this is incorrect. I believe, there is another way. Firstly, the statements found in Straight Tantra that there is no such thing as Gay Tantra are based on Straight people observing the energy of Gay people and forming their own conclusions about how the energy of Gay people *works*. But isn't that the same as a man giving advice to a woman about her periods, or about the practicalities of child birth?

His words would be just coming from theory, lacking any practical or personal experience.

What if these Straight conclusions about Gay energy anatomy are 'incomplete' because it was drawn up by people who did not fully understand the energy... and who did not need to, because it is not their own?

In the novel *Dune* by Frank Herbert, there is an energy space into which the female, matriarchal *Bene Gesserit* guild cannot look and so it is closed and alien to them. It is only men, in the form of the young Paul Atreides as the *Kwisatz Haderach*, who can look into that space and understand it. What if there is a similar space within Gay energy anatomy where Straight people cannot look, or even understand, because it is so *different* and *unique*? And why would Straight Tantra develop Gay Tantra anway? There is no point for Straight Tantra to develop Gay Tantra... because it would be of no use to them.

But often in the inner world, it is only when you walk the path do you *really* get to understand how something *really* works, what is *really* going on. A man standing at the bottom of a mountain, with a pair of binoculars, can possibly look up and trace a potential route up to the top of the mountain. But only a man climbing that route will come to know if it can really reach the top, and what the benefits and pitfalls are.

So it is possible that Chinese energy medicine, mostly practised by Straight men, looking in from the 'outside', and without the personal 'need' to investigate further, have jumped to 'conclusions'... and left it at that... for thousands of years. But when you look *deeper*... when you *have* to walk the path because it is *your life*... you find an unexpected door opens before you... and the path takes you into a whole new and miraculous dimension.

Also, in the field of medicine over the last hundred years, there have been many examples of doctors and scientists thinking they 'knew' how the human body worked… only to find they have got it *so wrong*. For decades, science preached that, after childhood, the brain was hard-wired for life, and it was impossible for the brain to re-wire itself. However, back in 1968 a scientist called Michael Merzenich, conducted a series of experiments which proved the exact opposite. He had stumbled across *neuroplasticity*, and we now know that the human brain is constantly updating itself, although the process does slow down the older we get, and this discovery has opened up whole new possibilities in terms of our understanding of the brain and new forms of physical and psychological treatments.

But these treatments would not have been possible if the traditional medical and scientific orthodoxy (i.e. 'the brain cannot re-write itself') had continued and crushed this new insight to death (because the people in power didn't want to admit they had been wrong, didn't want to appear to have been foolish or misguided).

There is the belief that a change in any paradigm goes through three distinct phases. First the new insight is *ignored*, then it is *ridiculed*, and then, only when it can no longer be ignored and ridiculed, is it finally *accepted*. But, from what I have observed, this is also a generational process. It is only when the old-guard, the ones who have an active investment in the old paradigm, have retired or died-off, that the new paradigm can really take root.

It also used to be believed that stomach ulcers were caused by stress, and anyone who believed different was shouted down by the medical community as 'heretics'. However, thanks to a brave and committed doctor from Australia, Barry Marshall (he won a Nobel prize for his work in 2005), it has now been found that stomach ulcers are caused by bacteria, and can be cured with a simple course of antibiotics. But he had to fight long and hard, against prejudice and scientific ridicule, before people started to recognise the truth of what he had discovered.

According to the historian Daniel Boorstin, "The greatest obstacle to knowledge isn't ignorance; it is the illusion of knowledge." So if this is occurring in the world of science and medicine even now... Why should we assume that everything passed down through our spiritual and energy traditions is absolutely 100% correct (... and also correct for all time)? Especially when it was written by Straight people about Gay energy anatomy?

Let's compare two pieces of 'information'.

• Do not stick your finger into a live electric socket, your physical body cannot handle the resulting electrical current, and you will hurt yourself, you may even die.

• According to the ancient Jain tradition, a woman cannot obtain enlightenment, or *moksha*. If a woman wants to obtain to enlightenment she will need to be re-born as a man, and continue with her spiritual pursuit in that lifetime.

The question is... which one do you believe is *true*?

Obviously, the first one is correct. Our physical bodies are not designed to process a significant amount of electricity, and we will harm ourselves if we try.

And the second one... to the Western mind is a lot of 'bullshit'. But, the important thing to realise is that, thousands of years ago, people did believe that to be true... because that is what their spiritual tradition preached as being *the truth*. So people organised their lives according to this truth, men were obviously more spiritually evolved, and women were taught to know their true place in the scheme of things. But this belief also begs the question 'Why would a Soul want to incarnate into the body of a woman if there was no possibility of spiritual progress?' It would mean that half the human population was a spiritual dead end.

One of the things which I believe is very important when wading through religious and spiritual beliefs and texts is to discern:

- Information which is based on scientific principles.

- Information which comes from cultural prejudice and bias.

Basically, it is the difference between what *will* harm you, and what you have been *told* will harm you, so you don't even go there and never come to understand whether it was right or wrong.

So if we return to Daniel Reid's statement that Gay male sexuality is 'harmful', we can look at it from two perspectives:

- It is a sound, scientific understanding, based on an understanding on how the Yang polarity works.

- It is a cultural prejudice, which arises from a) prejudice against Gay males and, b) a lack of understanding of how Gay energy anatomy really works.

Now, which is right? Well, I'll let you decide that for yourself, after I have fully presented my case for the defence.

One of the things which I have learnt from Osho is that human consciousness is continually *evolving*, and new possibilities and opportunities within the field of human consciousness *can* occur. Therefore, what was right for people two thousand years ago may not be right for 'now', which means, over time, to stay fresh and relevant a spiritual tradition also needs to remain open to what is happening around it.

Finally, I cannot help but ask the question 'Why would a Soul want to incarnate into the body of a Gay man or woman if there was no possibility of spiritual progress?' If it was just a spiritual 'dead end'... there would be no point. And from what I have observed to date, everything a Soul does has a point (even if we can't always understand what that point may be).

So... What if... A Soul decides to incarnate into Gay bodies because they want to explore the whole Yin / Yang polarity *from a completely different perspective, from a different direction?*

But if that were true, then there would need to be an internal source of Yin within each Gay man, and an internal source of Yang within each Gay woman. Gay energy anatomy would have to be 'different' to Straight energy anatomy, and something 'uncharted' by the conventional / traditional energy systems we have to date.

I believe there is a 'clue' to the location of these internal sources of Yin and Yang in another of the world's ancient spiritual traditions.

Egyptian Alchemy.

The Egyptian tradition is no longer a living tradition, but it did cover 4,000 to 5,000 years of human history, and their mystics also knew a thing or two about human consciousness. In its time it was probably as vibrant as Tantra or Taoism.

The Egyptians were to the Greeks and Roman what Tibet is now to the West, and Egyptian alchemy later fed into the Greek and Western spiritual and mystery traditions. Pythagoras, the father of Western science and mysticism, is meant to have discovered his enlightenment while studying with the priests of an ancient, mystical Egpytian tradition.

Now we have to careful about drawing upon an old and dead 'mystical' tradition, especially one which was mainly oral, because so much has become lost to us. But I am *not* proposing that we try and resurrect Egyptian Alchemy... just borrow 'one single idea' from it. The great thing about Gay Polarity Tantra is that we are only drawing upon this one idea / concept, which was also part of popular Egyptian consciousness, so it was never considered 'top secret'. The rest of GPT comes from actual energy exploration and meditation in our current time period.

What is this idea?

It is the differentiation between the **Ka** and the **Khat**.

For the Egyptians, the Khat was the physical body, the physical self.

The Ka was an energy duplicate of the physical self which walked alongside the Khat during this lifetime... That is *all* we are going to draw from Egyptian Alchemy, that's *all* we need (actually, no, there is one other small thing we'll need, but we'll come to that a bit later).

The Ka is very similar to the Western esoteric tradition of the 'etheric double'. It is believed that the Ka, or 'etheric double', is tied to the physical self and yet also has an independent existence. It is the energy duplicate, or template, of the physical self. We can even go a little further and say that the Ka has a personality of its own, which is different and separate from the Khat, or the physical self. But the Khat is dependent on the Ka, because the energy body supports the physical body.

At this point, we're defining the Individual as being what manifests in this lifetime, and the Soul as everything else 'beyond' the current individual (and remember, there is a whole, multi-dimensional universe all around us), and we're not getting too caught up in the different possible levels and subtle bodies.

The next diagram shows this relationship:

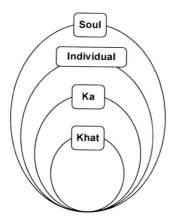

Figure 1: Soul, Ka & Khat

So in our explorations, we have now added an extra 'body' to the equation. This extra body, the Ka, is one which everyone will have – Straight Male, Straight Female, Gay Male and Gay Female.

To build on this, we now need to discuss the nature of *polarity*, and the difference between *Yin* and *Yang*, which we will do in our next chapter.

Final Thought:

Some of you may be asking the question 'Why doesn't the Tantric, or Taoist traditions, also refer to the Ka and Khat?'

My answer... Why indeed? But then... Why didn't the Ancient Chinese discover the chakra system... or why didn't the Ancient Indians discover the meridian system? I mean, it's not as if both cultures didn't have lots of people meditating and 'looking' around inside over thousands of years.

The only answer I can give is that just as an individual goes into the 'storehouse of all knowledge' and only focuses on what they are attracted to and resonate with, and I believe it must also work this way on a larger, cultural level. Over time, the Chinese tradition came to focus on the meridian system, and so everything else became 'invisible' to them, while the Indians focused solely on the chakra system, and the Egyptians on their system of subtle bodies. It's only now, that the cultural boundaries are being broken down in our modern world that the *entirety* of this information is coming into shared consciousness.

That's the best way I have found to explain it.

C9. Yin & Yang:

Over the millennia, the ancient Chinese sages developed and refined the energy concepts we know today as *Yin* and *Yang* to help understand the world of *polarity*.

Now other ancient spiritual systems also developed similar concepts to understand / describe polarity, but the Yin / Yang model will be the one we use in this book, as it is probably the most well-defined and useful of all the world's 'polarity' systems.

The concept of Yin and Yang was discovered in China, probably around the 14th Century B.C., arising from Chinese sages and philosophers observing the working of the natural universe around them, but also the working of those same natural forces *within* themselves.

In his book *Archetypal Acupuncture*, Gary Dolowich writes that:

> *The concept of Tao corresponds to the unity underlying all existence... According to ancient wisdom, this model based on the number two enables us to make comparisons and discern "the movements of all creation." Everything can be said to be yin or yang, relative to its polar complement. Thus we can contrast dark and light, night and day, cold and hot, water and fire, rest and movement, falling and rising, feminine and masculine – each pair representing a yin/yang relationship. Neither is seen as more valuable than the other...[1]*

For the Taoist sages of China, and the later Zen masters, if you do not understand how Yin and Yang come together to manifest your life, then you are fated to be trapped within a repeating cycle, literally being endlessly passed between hate and love, dark and light, death

---

[1]   Gary Dolowich, page 41 to 42.

and life.

However, if you *do* understand, and so can work with the flow of Yin and Yang, then it is possible to live a happy and contented life, even riding this natural wave to achieve enlightenment itself.

For example, Sosan, the 3rd Zen Patriarch writes in his *Book of True Faith (Xin Xin Ming)*:

> *The Great Way isn't difficult for those who are unattached to their preferences.*
> *Let go of longing and aversion, and everything will be perfectly clear.*
> *When you cling to a hairbreadth of distinction, heaven and earth are set apart.*
> *If you want to realize the truth, don't be for or against.*
> *The struggle between good and evil is the primal disease of the mind.[2].*

So it's really all a question of 'perspectives'.

To perceive the 'all that is', an individual needs to set aside their mind which analyses, divides and defines, i.e. the *Yin / Yang mind*. But to function in our manifest world of form, that same individual needs to work with Yin and Yang, we need to analyse, define and identify the distinctions between different 'things'. In the manifest world, we need our Yin / Yang mind to function successfully. So it is a question of 'what side of the fence' your consciousness is currently exploring (or as the spiritual teacher Duane Packer calls it 'being level appropriate').

As Gary Dolowich pointed out earlier, Yin is associated with the

---

2   From Sosan's *Hsin Hsin Ming (The Book of Nothing)*. He was the 3rd Patriarch of Zen Buddhism. From, *The Enlightened Heart: An Anthology of Sacred Poetry*, edited by Stephen Mitchell. I know that there are some scholars who dispute whether Sosan is the true author of this work... but in this book, I am assuming he was.

'yielding', with water, with the female, with winter, with night. In contrast, Yang is associated with the 'assertive', with fire, with the male, with summer, with day.

But fundamentally, Yin is perceived as a force which 'holds and nurtures', while Yang is perceived as a force which 'flows'. Therefore:

• Summer is believed to be more Yang, as the energy is expansive and flowing during this season, while winter is considered more Yin, because the energy sinks down into the ground, where it is held, nurtured and re-charged by the earth before the start of the New Year.

• Organs / meridians are classified as more Yin or Yang based on this system. The Heart and Kidney are Yin, because their function is hold and contain, whereas the Small Intestine and Large Intestine are Yang, because they require more flow to function correctly.

Basically if something / someone is too Yin, then energy cannot flow and becomes stuck, but if something / someone is too Yang, then there is too much flow, which can be just as dangerous.

Within Yin / Yang theory, it is the 'tension' between these two polar opposites which creates a flow of energy, or *chi*, between them, as shown in the diagram below.

Without the polarity of Yin and Yang, there would be no tension, no flow, no energy or chi, and the manifest universe could not continue, or even exist.

But in practical terms, nothing which 'manifests' is purely composed of only Yin or only Yang. Everything, every person, is a mixture of the two. A man is said to be more Yang then Yin, a woman is said to be more Yin then Yang.

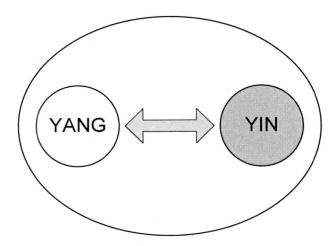

Figure 2: Yin & Yang

But if you take it down to the 'individual' level, then different men will have different percentage mixes of these two polarities, and the same is true for women. Some men have more Yin then others, and so come across as more feminine, while some women have more Yang, and so come across as more masculine. Some men are very masculine, while some women are very feminine. The astrological signs in which the 10 main planets fall in a natal chart show the exact yin / yang ratio for each individual, regardless of their gender.

However, it is important to realise that just because a man has more Yin then other men, or a woman more Yang then other women, does not equate to them being 'homosexual'. I have come across feminine men / masculine women who are heterosexuals in happy and long-standing relationships with their partners.

The trick is to be born into a culture, and a time in human history, where being a feminine man, or a masculine woman, is not a problem. Unfortunately, the whole yin / yang dynamic may also be expressed differently through different cultures, societies and time-periods, and so this may not always be possible.

We human beings tend to prefer simple rules which we can live our lives by, simple equations which show us how the universe works. But the mistake we can then make, and which others often exploit, is that in our yearning for the simple we *over-simplify*, which then leads to a whole host of problems.

Yin and Yang is a very simple concept, but the way these two forces interact can create of whole world of different combinations and permutations (in Taoism, this is often referred to as the '10,000 things')... many of which exist beyond what many people would consider to be *tidy* or *acceptable*.

For example, it's not always the case of a beneficial Yin / Yang ratio being 50 / 50. There are times when 50 / 50 is actually too much Yang and more Yin is required to safely balance out and contain the Yang, so it's more a 80 / 20. For example, when a baby is conceived and develops in the womb, you can divide the time period into a Yang phase and a Yin phase. If you define the Yang phase as being from ejaculation to the embryo attaching to the womb wall (3 to 5 days, depending on how fast those 'little swimmers' move), and the Yin phase as starting from this point on towards the actual birth (nine months), then you can see that more Yin is required then Yang to safely stabilize and nurture the growing embryo. In fact, if you were to introduce more Yang into the womb during pregnancy it might be too destructive, and actually kill off the baby. A burst of Yang is required to get the process started, but then Yin needs to take over, and Yang needs to take a back seat.

This isn't just the case during pregnancy. When manifesting a project or situation, people often put too much Yang in to the process overall, and so 'overcook' it. This is because they equate Yin with 'nothing happening' and are not comfortable with being *patient*. But there are times when you need for Yin to take over, to come in and nurture and stabilize things. When manifesting I have found 80 / 20 is usually a good rule of thumb.

Interestingly, in Chinese philosophy, not all schools totally agree on the exact nature of Yin and Yang.

Just consider the famous Yin / Yang symbol, where Black is Yin, and White is Yang.

Figure 3: Yin / Yang 1

What most Westerners usually miss is that there are two versions of this famous symbol, and the other version of this famous symbol is shown below.

Figure 4: Yin / Yang 2

As you can see, the first symbol is plain black versus white, while the second version of the symbol has a small white dot in the centre of the black, with a small black dot in the centre of the white.

Why are there two versions? Because each symbol is used by different schools within Taoism, and pictorially represent their differences of opinion.

The second symbol is used by the Chinese school which believes that if you push Yin to an extreme it will change into Yang, and if you push Yang to an extreme it will change into Yin. The symbol therefore represents the little bit of Yin hidden within Yang, and vice versa.

However, there is another school of Chinese philosophy which totally rejects this view, and they conceive of Yin and Yang as being two totally opposing forces, diametrically set apart, and for them it is fundamentally impossible for one to change into the other. This is why their symbol, the first one, lacks the two central dots.

Now, to confuse things, I think they're 'both' right. To try and explain this, I have come to believe that Yin is like *magnetism*, and Yang is like *electricity*. Each force is completely separate and unique, and yet on some deeper level, which science doesn't fully understand yet, they are both 'linked together' in a unified force we know as *electromagnetism*. If you pass an electric current along a copper wire, a magnetic field is created around the wire. And if you pass a copper wire through a magnetic field, then an electric current instantly starts to flow along the copper wire. This is one of the scientific mysteries which make our modern world possible, and is at the heart of the electric motor, and other pieces of modern technology.

Based on this analogy, I believe *Yin* and *Yang* are separate and opposed, but at the same time they can also interact and create more of the other 'pole'. In fact, you could make the argument that, within our physical universe, Yin 'is' magnetism, and Yang 'is' electricity.

But there are two interesting things which arise from this:

- Scientifically, it is possible to create electro-magnetic fields where there is more electricity (Yang), and ones where there is more magnetism (Yin), as well as ones which are balanced (Yin + Yang).

- In the basic experiment mentioned above, where electricity creates magnetism, and magnetism creates electricity, the common factor is *movement.*

So, I would argue that the first symbol is a description / understanding of Yin and Yang in isolation, and in a universe where there is little or no movement. In a sense this is 'pure' Yin and Yang. However, the more movement you introduce, the more Yin and Yang interact, the more Yin and Yang is created, which is better described in the second symbol. And we also need to remember that this polarity creates *chi,* the energy flowing between Yin and Yang, which means the more movement occurring between Yin and Yang the more *chi* is created.

But what has any of this to do with Gay Tantra? We're getting to that. But be patient for a little while longer... we've almost reached the important bit.

Now the key thing about Yin / Yang theory is that Yin is a holding / containing force, while Yang is a flowing / expansive force, and together the two complement each other so that things can manifest and evolve.

I currently believe that, although there are times when Yin and Yang have to do their own thing (i.e. flow versus contain), when they are balanced 50 / 50 this creates the maximum amount of potential chi. However when there is more Yin, that chi is held and nurtured, but when there is more Yang, that chi flows more easily. But when there is too much Yin, the chi becomes stuck and stagnates, and when there is too much Yang, the chi flows too fast and becomes destructive. This would mean, if Yin = magnetism and Yang = electricity, then chi is something else, flowing within and through these electro-magnetic fields.

So a woman is considered to be *more Yin*, because she has a womb, which can safely hold and nurture the baby, whereas a man is *more Yang* because he has a penis, which is designed to shoot sperm up into the womb. A healthy womb need to 'hold and contain', while a healthy penis needs to 'flow and shoot'.

But now we're coming back to the earlier quote from Daniel Reid, where Gay male couples are considered to be *too Yang*, where there is too much flow, too much assertive energy, whereas Gay female couples are considered to be *too Yin*, too much holding / yielding, not enough flow.

And I do understand and get what Chinese energy medicine is arguing here…

When a man has sex, the sperm in his testicles vibrate, which creates a powerful electro-magnetic field (Yang dominant), which in heterosexual relationships is held, contained and transformed by the woman's vagina / womb (Yin dominant). For Straight couples, their two polarities together balance out these extreme energies, and a powerful flow of chi is created in the 'between'.

However, if you put two Gay men together and they engage in sex, then you have two sets of testicles, generating two powerful electro-magnetic fields (both Yang dominant), but they lack a Yin container to hold / transform this energy… so any chi created could possibly become destructive to those two individuals. In contrast, because the electro-magnetic field generated by two Gay women engaging in sex is Yin dominant, it will be much less dangerous, although it may possibly lead to a loss or stagnation of energy. And, because with the Gay male couple it is Yang / Yang, and with Gay female couple it is Yin / Yin, there is less beneficial chi being generated anyway, because chi is most efficiently generated from the difference between the polarity of Yin and Yang.

So I do understand the reason why Chinese energy medicine believes that homosexuality is a problem. I am not ignoring the potential danger. I do get what they are saying.

But what if... (Here it comes, the Big Idea behind Gay Polarity Tantra) What if... *The difference between Gays and Straights isn't just a question of the polarity of their physical body, the Khat, but also the polarity of their energy body, the etheric double, the Ka?*

What if for Straight Men the polarity of the Khat and Ka is both the same – Yang. And for a Straight Woman the polarity of the Khet and Ka is also the same – Yin.

But what if... for Gay people... the polarity of their Khet and Ka is not the same?

What if for Gay Men, their Khat is Yang, while their Ka is Yin? What if for Gay Women, their Khat is Yin, while their Ka is Yang? What if Gay Men and Women do have an internal source of Yin / Yang, it's just that we're all wired differently from Straight individuals, as shown in the diagram below. (I know I have left out Bisexuals as a specific polarity type. They do exist, but we'll be discussing them in a later chapter.)

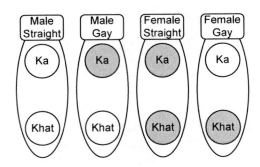

Figure 5: 4 Polarity Types

And also... what if the *distance* between the Khet and Ka can be different for different Gay individuals, perhaps even overlapping, as shown in the diagram below?

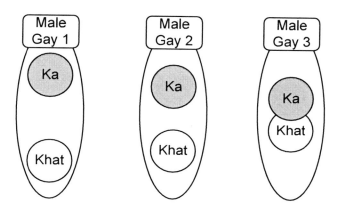

Figure 6: Ka & Khat Distance

This would mean that for some Gay people they come across as very straight (i.e. their Khat and Ka is further apart), while others come across as more *metrosexual* (i.e. their Khat and Ka is closer together, possibly overlapping). So their physical body expresses more of their feminine or masculine 'energy' side. This distance wouldn't matter as much for a Straight individual, because they would just come across as being more 'male' or more 'female' (which is usually socially acceptable). But for a Gay person it would make a big difference, as it would impact upon the way their personality is expressed and perceived.

Now, I know this is big assumption to make, but as with any theory, I believe it can 'proved':[3]

---

3   Without supporting proof through the completion of a real-life experiment, the theory remains that, only a theory.

• If it helps us to better explain how the Universe works, and this can be shown through direct observation and inner experience.

• If it can be shown to be true through actual and repeatable physical 'experiments'.

Therefore, I am not proposing anything here which I do not believe I cannot back up with:

• A better understanding of how the whole Gay / Straight thing works

• Practical 'energy experiments / experiences' which can open the door on a workable Gay Tantra that successfully solves the polarity issue

A huge boast I know, but I wouldn't be writing this book if I didn't think I could deliver.

However... the Tao has also put me into a corner where I have to write this book. But then I have also come to believe that, at the start of the 21st Century, the Tao wants this matter 'sorted' and so has had a hand in this from the start.

If the polarity of the Ka is indeed different to the Khat for Gay people, then this opens up Gay people to a whole new world of exciting possibilities... which we shall start to outline in our next chapter.

C10. Putting It All Together - The Big Picture:

In the last few chapters, I proposed two Big Ideas, which I suggested are the foundation for Gay Polarity Tantra.

Once again, these are:

> • <u>Idea 1</u>: Each individual has a physical self (Khat) and an energy self (Ka).

> • <u>Idea 2</u>: For a Straight individual the polarity of their Khat and Ka will be identical and the same as their physical gender, but for a Gay individual, the polarity of their Khat and Ka will be different, and the Ka will be the opposite of their physical gender.

Now, when combined, these two ideas present us with four possible polarity individual types:

- • Individual Type 1: Straight Male

- • Individual Type 2: Straight Female

- • Individual Type 3: Gay Male

- • Individual Type 4: Gay Female

For the moment, we are not going to include Bisexual Men and Women in our discussion. They will be covered in a later chapter.

Now, in this chapter, we are going to use the diagram below as our template, and explore how each of these individual types interact, on an energy level, with all the other types.

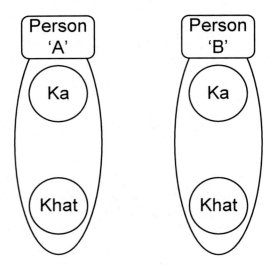

Figure 7: Template for All Energy Polarity Types

But in doing so, we are also going to include our 3rd new idea, the concept of an 'energy line'.

An energy line can potentially exist between any of the two Khats or two Kas, as is shown in our next diagram.

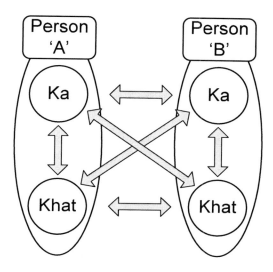

Figure 8: 6 Potential Energy Lines

As you can see, there are a total of 6 energy lines which can potentially exist between any two individuals.

Of these 6 potential energy lines:

• 2 of these energy lines exist totally within each individual (*vertical*).

• 2 of these energy lines exist between the two Khats and the two Kas (*horizontal*).

• 2 of these energy lines exist between the Khat and the opposing Ka (*diagonal*).

But for our 4 individual types, the potential combinations between a Khat and Ka, whether Yin or Yang, means only a *maximum* of 4 energy lines can exist at any one time, in any of the relationships we are about to explore... and in some relationships the number of energy lines is much less.

It all depends on the polarity which exists between the two individuals, between their respective Khats and Kas, it all depends on the set-up of their Yin and Yang.

Earlier we stated that chi flows between the polarity of Yin and Yang, which creates an 'attraction' energy line.

However, between Yang and Yang, or Yin and Yin, there is no flow of chi, and so no 'attraction' can exist, instead we have a 'repulsive' energy line.

For example, let us look at the energy relationship between a Gay Female and a Straight Male, as shown in the following diagram.

Note: In all our diagrams in this chapter, Yin is 'grey', and Yang is 'white'.

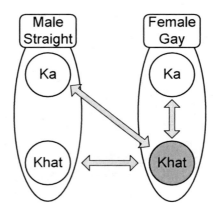

Figure 9: Gay Female / Straight Male

In this situation, there are three 'attractive' energy lines between:

- The Khat of the Gay Female and the Khat of the Straight Male (*horizontal*).

- The Khat of the Gay Female and the Ka of the Straight Male (*diagonal*).

- The Khat and Ka of the Gay Female (*vertical*).

However, everywhere else, there are only repulsive energy lines (which we will not be showing in our diagrams... But trust me, they are there). So, in this example, the Ka of the Gay Female, and the Ka of the Straight Male will be repulsive, and will attempt to push each other away, or if this is not possible, they may turn aggressive.

Now, we are not saying that *all* relationships between a Gay Female and a Straight Male will be the same... because family history, cultural influence, social standing, and personal karma will all play their part in moulding each relationship... and so each such relationship will be different and unique. But each pair of individuals in such a relationship cannot help but express the above energy dynamic to some extent, and so we can therefore use it as an archetype to understand the deeper levels of this type of relationship.

As we have already said, chi will only flow between Yin and Yang, as Yin needs to help stabilize and expand Yang, while Yang needs to activate and mobilize Yin. The possibility of Gay Tantra can therefore only exist where there is an 'attractive' energy line between Yin and Yang on some level... and if you can activate *all* 4 energy lines then great, you're definitely on to something... and this is also the same for Straight Tantra.

So we are now going to explore how Yin and Yang sets-up (or doesn't) between the Khat and Ka of the different individual types, whether

Straight or Gay. One of the things which is central to Gay Polarity Tantra is that *true* fulfilment only occurs between partners, whether heterosexual or homosexual, when all 4 'units' are fully engaged, which means both Khats and both Kas are connected up in some way.

This is not to say, as we shall see, that a 'relationship' is not possible if only three or two units are engaged. But it does mean that one or more of the units will not be present in the relationship, and will be effectively shut out, and so the potential for complete, 100% fulfilment cannot be achieved. Usually, it will be the Kas which are shut out of the relationship, and so there will be a nagging doubt, a feeling deep within, that there is something *missing*. However, because the Khat's are 'physically present' they are able to override these feelings, and continue in the way they want. In comparison, Kas have less control over the physical, and can only influence this arena.

Finally, there is also something which I have often read about in the Taoist sexual tradition, that when a man and women fully engage their sexual energies to work together, they have access to four times the energy then if they were to work alone. I have often wondered, why four times? Why not two? Or three?

But I now realise that when two people come together, and they are in true energy resonance, they also start to access their two Kas... which means the energy of 2 Khats + 2 Kas = 4.

PART THREE

But one thing we can be perfectly sure of is that life will never serve us in our search for some lasting sense of superiority. Life is oneness. It gives, then takes, has no liking for special consideration. And with those who are the most neglected, rejected, abused: there is where the greatest reality always lies hidden.

Peter Kingsley

A Story Waiting to Pierce You

C11. About Hammers, Fractals & Skyscrappers

When a friend of mine was reviewing an early draft of this book, her comment was, 'Great book... but be careful that you don't come across as too dogmatic'. So out came my Oxford Dictionary and I looked up the definition of 'dogmatic', just to be on the safe side:

Dogmatic: 1) Given to asserting or imposing personal opinions; 2) intolerantly authorative.

Which took me aback a little, as being dogmatic was something I definitely didn't want to be accused of, especially as in this book occasionally I am accusing others of being too dogmatic themselves... I mean it would hypocritical in the extreme. I would just be re-placing one dogma with another. However, upon reflection, and further discussion with my friend, I came to see what she was referring too, and this is why the current chapter has been included in this book, to provide a broader context, a wider perspective, for the information I am presenting.

Let me explain. Below is a diagram which outlines the two levels of polarity that influence each human being, their personality, behaviour and actions.

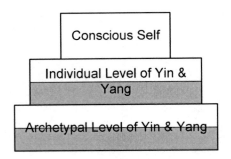

Figure 10: The Polarity Pyramid

There is an *individual level*, and beneath that there is an *archetypal level*. Each level is composed of different ratios of Yin and Yang, and the flow of chi / energy created between these two opposing polarities. These two levels are separate and distinct, and depending on how the energies set-up for an indivdual at birth, they can either complement or contradict each other. The levels can either pull in the same direction, or they can pull in opposite directions. They can either support each other, or they can be antagonistic.[1]

This is one of the reasons why each human being is so unique, because it is not just a question of the ratio of Yin & Yang on one level, but of the ratio on each of these two distinct levels, and also on how those two different and distinct levels *interact*.

That's the quick and easy way to explain it... but now I am going to explain it via the long route... the path not often taken... and let's see if we can pick up a little more information about this dual polarity phenonmenon along the way.

Figure 11: Children's Wooden Toy

---

1   In terms of human subtle anatomy, the *individual level* relates to the meridian system, while the *archetypal level* relates to the extra-ordinary vessels which lie below and energetically support the meridians.

Above is a photograph of a game for young children, where the child has to fit the right shape into the right hole. As adults we all know that it is impossible to put the wrong shape in the wrong hole, no matter how hard we struggle, or how hard we hit the block with our wooden hammer... although we only know this fact because we learnt it the hard way as a young child playing with a toy such as this.

A similar thing can happen with theoreticians, especially of the soft sciences. They have a theory to explain a particular phenomenon involving human beings, which predicts how a particular group of human beings will behave. However, does the theory arise from carefully observing human beings and their behaviour, which is the equivalent of working out which shape goes successfully goes into which hole? Or do they blindly assume they know how humans will behave, regardless of the hard evidence or what the actual humans might think. This is the equivalent of trying to hammer a square block into a circular hole, only with people instead of wooden blocks.

This is one of the motivations behind the birth of NLP (Neuro-Linguistic Programming) back in the 1960s, as a reaction to all the beautiful and exquisite psychological and human development theories which were totally unable to help a single human being improve their siuation... although they were still be taught in Universities by lecturers with a vested interest and secured tenure. In contrast, the creators of NLP, Richard Bandler and John Grinder had the revolutionary idea to study therapists, such as Milton Erickson and Virginna Starr, who were actually creating positive results for their clients, regardless of what any academic theory might say.

When a theoretician likes the sound of their own voice too much, and becomes divorced from real world results, then their theory can easily turn into dogma, where the theoretician imposes their own personal opinion onto an individual or group, saying this is how you all behave, but where the individual or group being studied turns around and says, no, we don't, that is just your opinion, and you are just plain wrong.

My friend felt that the theory proposed in the next ten chapters, Energy Polarity Types 1 to 10, was probably too simplistic to include all the possible nuisances and quirks of human behaviour.

And I can see where she is coming from with this, however, my counter-argument is that in these next ten chapters, I am explaining the ten archetypal energies out of which all human behaviour emerges, and I am focusing on the lowest level of the polarity pyramid, *the archetypal level*.

For example, below is an image of a fractal, which shows a very complex and beautiful design.

Figure 12: A Fractal

According to the website *Fractal Foundation*:

> Fractals are infinitely complex patterns that are self-similar across different scales. They are created by repeating a simple process over and over in an ongoing feedback

loop. Driven by recursion, fractals are images of dynamic systems – the pictures of Chaos.[2]

With a fractal it is possible to create amazing and beautiful patterns through repeating a simple process over and over again, on different levels, and this is something which is found throughout Nature. For example, this sea shell in the photograph below, which is somewhat similar to the fractal image above.

Figure 13: A Sea-shell

Snowflakes and leaves (see photograph below) also incorporate a fractal design. It is believed that Nature prefers to use fractal designs and patterns wherever possible because it is a very efficient way of generating shape and form.

---

2   http://fractalfoundation.org/resources/what-are-fractals

Figure 14: A Leaf

However, the power of fractals is not just confined to forms in the Natural world. It is also believed to underlie the whole Natural world itself, and this belief is found in several spiritual traditions. For example, in Taoism, there is a saying which goes:

The Tao creates Yin & Yang,
Yin & Yang creates the 5 Elements,
And the Five Elements create the 10,000 things.

Which is the Taoist way of saying that our manifest Universe is created out of simple and basic laws... the 10,000 things is 'everything that exists', which are 'created by repeating a simple energetic process over and over in an ongoing feedback loop... which is very fractal. In Taoism, the Eight Trigram energies are expressed through the eight extra-ordinary vessels, and the Five Element energies are expressed through the twelve meridians, and together they both create and support the whole of our individual personality. These combined energies are the source of our uniqueness.

A limited number of simple and distinct energetic patterns, dancing and interacting, creating an infinite number of forms and beings, creating the whole manifest Universe, creating the 7 billion plus human beings on this planet, each one with a different face and unique personality. So in the next ten chapters, with Energy Polarity Types 1 to 10, we will be exploring the 10 archetypal energies which motivate human behaviour from beneath. But these are largely forces which act on an individual from the archetypal level, and so many individuals are totally oblivious to their influence on their daily life.

There is another way to explain this whole multi-layered Yin / Yang phenonmenon, to view these archetypal energies from a different perspective. For example, below is a photograph of two skyscrapers from New York, U.S.A.

Figure 15: City Skyscrapers

This is how we are used to our buildings looking, all rising, soaring, smooth walls of stone and glass. But this is not what gives these buildings their shape, and this is definitely not what gives these buildings their strength. If we were to roll back the clock to the time when these skyscrapers were first being erected, they would look more like the photograph below.

Figure 16: Steel frame for constructing a tall building

All skyscrapers start out as a frame of steel girders, a steel cage around which the building is then built. As construction proceeds, the builders install the walls, floors and ceilings, the electrics, the plumbing, and after the building is given over to the owners, the building is turned into a hotel, a hospital, fitted out as a department store, or private apartments... and when that is done, the steel frame around which the building has been built is completely *hidden*, even though it still continues to provide the building with its fundamental strength and structure.

To a large extent, the same is true for each unique personality, which is built upon and around the *archetypal level*, and is an expression of one of the 10 Energy Polarity Types. Eventually, this archetypal level is completely covered by the *individual level*, which is what each person experiences as they live their life. For most people, these archetypal forces are buried deep within them, and the only time they ever become aware of them is a) if they consciously journey within, or b) these forces suddenly erupt up into their life in some way, rather like an earthquake which shakes the building at its core.

And for our third explanation... We can also see this phenonmenon at work within the domain of Astrology. For example, most people check out the reading for their star sign in their daily newspaper, but don't take it too seriously, because how can it speak to them when it applies equally to every individual born on that same day. The whole thing is far too simplistic. For them, astrology is just a bit of fun, light relief.

But newspaper astrology is only a small slice of the ancient art of Astrology, and only focuses on one planet, the Sun, but if you ever get to explore a full astrological natal chart, like the one for Albert Einstein, given below:

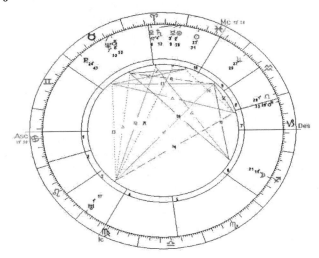

Figure 17: Einstein's Astrological Natal Chart (11.30 AM, 14th March 1879, Ulm, Germany)

You will find that astrology isn't just a matter of your Sun sign, there are nine other planets to also consider, plus the four angles, the twelve signs, and the twelve houses.

In fact, it is said that the *moment* of your birth, the pattern which is displayed through your natal chart, will not be repeated again for another 22,000 years. You are that unique... and according to astrology, your unique pattern is created from the relative positions of just 10 archetypal forces.

The other interesting thing about our astrological chart is that it can reveal the balance of Yin / Yang being expressed through our unique personality, which in Gay Polarity Tantra, is also known as our Khat. So your astrological chart can show you how Yin / Yang set-ups on the *individual level* of your unique personality.

But this is where we come to the problem with Gay Polarity Tantra if we just restrict it to the *archetypal level* and do not include the *individual level*. Basically, the theory becomes too simplistic if it was just restricted to the archetypal level. To understand any human being as a unique expression we need to explore **both** Yin / Yang levels, the *individual* and *archetypal*.

As we said earlier, if you explore the *individual level*, then you will observe that different men have different percentage mixes of these two polarities, and the same is true for women. Some men have more Yin then others, and so come across as more feminine, while some women have more Yang, and so come across as more masculine. Some men are very masculine, while some women are very feminine, and physical genitalia is not always a good or true indication of how masculine or feminine any person will be in their personality and expression.

To explain this, let's look at two of the Energy Polarity types which we shall be exploring in later chapters. The first occurs between two Straight Females:

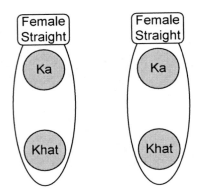

Energy Polarity Type 18: Straight Female to Straight Female

In this Polarity Type, no attraction is possible between the Kas and Khats of these two individuals, because they all Yin. Or at least it is not possible on the *archetypal level*, which is what this diagram is describing.

But on the earth plane, no one can be 100% Yin or 100% Yang, and so each individual is a mixture of the two polarities... although the ratio between the two varies greatly between individuals, as we can see in the digram below, which now includes their two individual ratios to the side:

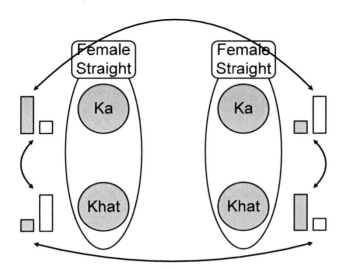

Figure 19: Energy Polarity Type 3: Straight Female to Straight Female **with ratios**

As before, on the *archetypal level* there is no attraction between the two Khats and two Kas.

However, on the *individual level* each of these two Straight Female now have different ratios of Yin & Yang (say 25% Yin & 75% Yang for the Khat on the left and 75% Yin & 25% Yang on the right). So now it is indeed possible to have an attraction between these two women. For these two specific Straight Females, on the *archetypal level*, there is no attraction, but on the *individual level* attraction is possible... although it will be down to their respective conscious selves, and their particular beliefs, as to whether that attraction is ever actioned.

Let's look at the Energy Polarity possible between a Straight Male and Gay Male:

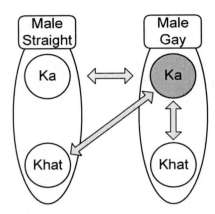

Figure 20: Energy Polarity Type 6 - Straight Male to Gay Male

When we come to Energy Polarity Type 6, and the energy relationship between a Straight Male and Gay Male, then the central arrows show the attractions which are possible at the *archetypal level*... and as we can see there are a number of attraction lines possible, especially between the two Kas, although not on the physical level between the two Khats (and we will discuss the implications of all this in the relevant chapter).

But once again, this whole picture can dramatically change once we add the Yin / Yang ratio for the *individual level*:

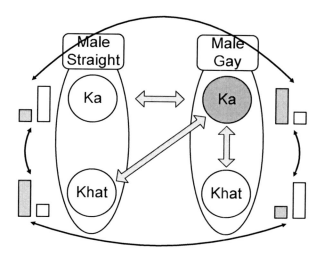

Figure 21: Energy Polarity Type 6 - Straight Male to Gay Male **with ratios**

If the Straight Male Khat is more Yin than Yang (i.e. 25% Yang, and 75% Yin), and the Gay Male Khat is more Yang than Yin (i.e. 75% Yang, and 25% Yin) then this will also change the whole energy dynamics between the two, and the 'individual' Gay Male will have a more aggressive Khat personality, and the Straight Male much less so (he will probably come across as more feminine).

Just think back a moment to the Battle of Battle of Chaeronea in 338 B.C. where 300 homosexual warriors fought to the death against the might of the Macedonian army under Phillip II. These men may have been Gay, but they were as brave and fearless as any Yang males come, which is probably why Phillip said over their dead bodies, 'Perish any man who suspects that these men either did or suffered anything unseemly.' Which was his way of saying that they died like 'real men', regardless of their sexual orientation... which for a Greek warrior was probably the highest compliment. After all, this was the Astrological age of Aries the Ram.

On the individual level, Gay men and woman come in all shape, sizes, and polarities, just as Straight men and women do.

So through looking at these two examples we can see that when you add the *individual Yin / Yang level* to the *archetypal level*, things can and do get much more interesting and complicated.

What I have come to believe is that we are actually dealing with different levels, the *individual* and the *archetypal*, one of which obscures the other, just as the steel girders of a skyscraper are obscured by the walls and glass on the outside.

Which brings us back, once again, to the pyramid of polarity levels.

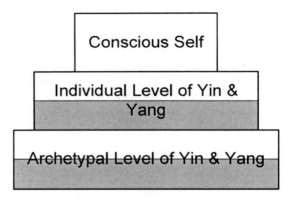

Figure 22: The Polarity Pyramid

In the 10 Energy Polarity chapters which follow next, we will be exploring the *archetypal level*, the 'steel girders' around which our personality is built... and this is an important level, because it shows us how our core energies function, it shows us what is driving us from a deep level, and helps explain many of the issues which occur between Men and Women, Straight and Gay, individually and culturally. But it is not the whole story, and if I were to have left it at that then my friend would have been correct, I would be failing into the trap of being too dogmatic.

*The 10 Energy Polarity types are **part** of the picture, but they are **not** the whole picture... and so if you cannot see yourself reflected in them, this is probably because you are more attuned to the Yin / Yang polarity being expressed through your individual level.*

But at the individual and archetypal levels, just like a fractal pattern, these two forces, Yin & Yang, and the different ratios which can occur between them, work together to manifest a whole univserse of different human personalities, just like each snowflake is original and unique... so many infinite possibilities that no book could ever include all the possible permutations.

Remember in Taoism they wisely say:

The Tao creates Yin & Yang,
Yin & Yang creates the 5 Elements,
And the Five Elements create the 10,000 things.

Final Note:

When exploring the two Energy Polartiy examples given in this chapter you may have noticed that the Yin ratio for the Ka is always the reverse of the Khat. So for an individual, if the Khat is 75% Yang and 25% Yin, then their Ka must be 25% Yang and 75% Yin.

From what I have observed and found, in both Straight and Gay people, on the individual level, the Ka is *always* a mirror and reverse of the polarity of the Khat... and if you think about it, this is probably a good thing. Because this means that on the *individual level*, there is always a connection, attraction and flow of energy between the Khat and the Ka, regardless of gender and sexual orientation. It is only when an individual delves down to the *archetypal level* that things start to change.

Admittedly, there is a Yin / Yang ratio even at the *archetypal level*, although it is very subtle, and doesn't manifest in the same way as that found at *individual level*. In fact, we don't have time in this current book to do justice to the subtleties of this archetypal level of Yin / Yang.

For the sake of our current discussion, it is therefore easier to treat the archetypal level for each person as being either Yin or Yang, and there is still a great deal of truth to be found in approaching them in this way. In contrast, the subtleties and nuances of the archetypal realm are only really relevent for someone who wishes to journey within and explore this particular inner realm of energy.

C12. Energy Polarity Type 1 - Straight Male & Straight Female:

The 1st Energy Polarity Type which we are going to explore is your traditional Straight Male and Straight Female scenario. They're the norm, they're everywhere... basically you can't avoid them. In fact, odds are, they probably gave birth to you.

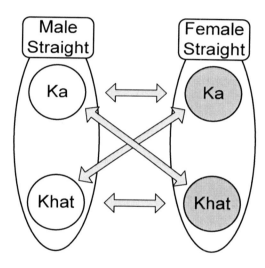

Figure 23: Straight Male to Straight Female

So with this energy scenario, the Khat and Ka of the Straight man are both Yang, and the Khat and Ka of the Straight woman are both Yin.

This means that energy can flow between:

- The two Khats on the physical level (*horizontal*).

- The two Kas on the energy level (*horizontal*).

- The Male's Khat and the Female's Ka (*diagonal*).

- .The Female's Khat and the Male's Ka (*diagonal*).

In this scenario, all 4 'units' are connected by energy lines, no unit is missed out, and so potentially this can be a fulfilling relationship. These four 'attractive' energy lines also create a Figure Eight shape (i.e. '8'), which is standing upright. So in this energy set-up Yin can fully stabilize and nurture Yang, while Yang can energise and mobilize Yin.

However, what is also interesting is that, within the each individual, there is no energy flow between their own Khat and Ka. In fact it is an *impossibility*. This means that each Straight individual does not have an internal source of their opposite polarity / energy, Yin or Yang, and so are totally dependent on their partners to help them create this energy and access this polarity. Literally, there is no constant / sustainable energy flow within their psyche between their individual Khat and Ka.

This may be why heterosexual cultures, throughout history, have placed so much emphasis upon the need for marriage, or some form of stable relationship between a man and woman, because:

- A Straight Male and Female can only develop their energies / personality through a relationship with their opposite polarity.

- Each party can only access the potential of their own Ka through the intervention of an external party of the 'opposite' gender. They cannot do so 'directly' (although we will discuss potential 'loopholes' to this statement a little later).[1]

---

1   Although the exact details of those marriages / relationships, the power dynamics within them, and the nature of the contract between the two parties, does vary considerably from culture to culture.

This also means that, from a Tantric point of view, Straight people are not really equipped for Solo Cultivation (i.e. using their own internal energy for personal and spiritual development, especially if they need to draw upon their own sexual energy). Perhaps this is the reason why the energetic relationship between the Khat and the Ka is given little or no mention in the Straight Tantric traditions. Within the context of Straight Tantra, the Ka remains mostly hidden, lost behind an energetic veil.

Within any Straight individual not only is there no energy flow between their Khat and Ka, instead there is actually a 'repulsive' energy line... and within some men, that repulsive force may also become quite *aggressive*. This may be one of the reasons why your average man is more sceptical / cynical about the possibility of their having a spiritual side, and about any mention of an inner world. Their Khat is aggressive towards their own inner Ka, even though it cannot directly see it, and wants to push it away or aside. Instead of turning within, the Straight male Khat prefers to focus on the external, materialistic world.

Indeed, the same words used earlier by Daniel Reid about Gay men could also be used about Straight men in this context. Within a Straight man, too much Yang (unless balanced by external Yin) can lead to psychological and physiological issues, because the different parts of their psyche can literally be pushed apart by the centrifugal forces of excessive Yang.

It is only when an individual's consciousness expands sufficiently enough to overcome this 'repulsion' that they become aware of their Ka, and seek to draw in enough Yin to achieve internal harmony and balance. But unless balanced by Yin, the Straight male spiritual path will always be prone to conflict, aggression, and imbalance, whether against the self or others.

That is why many so-called 'Holy Men' are quite happy to go to war against their particular version of the 'infidel'… but really it is excessive Yang 'talking'. Maybe this is why, on average, men tend to be more angry and aggressive then women.

Also, we must remember here that, although the norm is usually to establish energy lines with your 'loving' partner, for some women or men, who are in relationships which are all but dead, this is no longer possible… and so they often look around for an energetic substitute… and the closest people on hand is often their own sons and daughters.

Although these people are not engaging in actual physical incest, on an energetic level they are leaning upon their son's and daughter's energy field to provide them with the energy / polarity which their partner cannot or will not provide to them. However, they are doing their children a disservice in the long run, as it will most likely have a destabilising impact on their future relationships.

Another interesting twist with the Straight Male / Female scenario is found within the concept of *polygamy.* We stated earlier that there are times when the balance point isn't a question of Yin / Yang being 50 / 50, sometimes you need more Yin to hold, contain and balance the more fiery Yang, say 80 / 20. There are times when more Yin is required to put out a raging Yang fire.

In a long-term relationship, the Female's Yin is able to build up over time, which means it eventually reaches a level where it can comfortably hold and contain the Male's Yang. But for that to happen, Yin does need *time*… However, as a man becomes more Yin the older he gets, overtime the woman usually finds it easier to contain the energies of her partner.

There are cultures, societies and religions where a man taking more than one wife is considered socially acceptable, and there is certainly a sexual fantasy among many Straight men about sharing their bed with more than one woman. There will obviously be a 'macho ego' thing going on in these encounters, whether real or imagined.

However, it is possible that some Straight men may unconsciously seek multiple female partners as a way of 'grounding' their expansive Yang energy, especially when young. This may be something which is a necessity as the Yang builds within the young Straight male. Remember, a build-up of excessive Yang may actually be 'painful'... and will certainly lead to feelings of restlessness and frustration. It is interesting that, in modern Western societies, as young men have lost many of the traditional outlets for their Yang expansive / explosive energy, many have turned to sex as a way of grounding their Yang energy, turning away from committed, stable relationships, towards one night stands, multiple sexual encounters, and internet sex (where the female isn't even in the room).

In these encounters, Yang is being released, so there is some easing of the energetic tension for the Straight man, but because no formal relationship forms with a woman, her Yin cannot work its magic, and so nothing is being shared or transformed... and so the man has to move on to another woman for another 'temporary' fix / release.

If that man is part of a 'lads' or 'gang' culture then this will heat up their Yang energy even more, and this energy will then need to find an constant expression... either through aggressive behaviour, fighting or sex. But this is nothing new. War is a Yang activity, involving men fighting men. As conflict builds, more Yang is created, which has to be expressed through fighting... or the rape of women.

It is a terrible fact of war that the 'women of the fallen' often suffer at the hands of their male conquerors. This is partly a 'crushing the opposition' ego thing... but it will also be a massive discharge of Yang energy. Because remember... if Straight men cannot discharge this build-up of Yang energy then it will start to destroy them, pull them apart from the inside, on both a physiological and psychological level. Unconsciously, Straight men are continually looking for ways to discharge their excessive Yang energy.[2]

Not that I am a psychiatrist, or a trained mental health professional... However, if I were to presume to advise in these areas... One of the things I would be looking to do is *reduce* the Yang element within an individual's psyche... either through reducing the Yang, or increasing the Yin element influencing the mind. When people say 'He / She is tearing themselves apart'... it is Yang which is doing the 'tearing'... and for healing to occur these people need to be brought back into a state of inner balance.

But going back to our main question... we can now ask... 'Does this need for polygamy apply the other way around?' Would some women who are very Yin require more Yang than a single Straight man can provide to help stabilise her own energies? Probably. Indeed, for a few women, almost certainly.

There are a few societies around the women in which the Straight women did (sorry do, because they haven't died out completely yet) take more than one husband. It is conceivable that a few women have so much Yin that it becomes 'stuck' and cannot 'flow', and so they need a lot of Yang energy to get their chi flowing. It is conceivable that they may need to engage with more than one Straight male to do this.

However, the problems such a woman might encounter include:

- Too much Yin doesn't usually take the initiative, and so they will probably stay at home suffering, rather than go out a seek multiple partners (so you probably won't see these kind of women hanging around single's bars).

- Their culture and society may not support women acting in this way, portraying them as 'harlots' and 'slags'... although that

---

2   I believe sport may possibly be another such outlet. But then, I may be prejudiced here. When young, I was never too interested in sport.

same society may be quite happy with Straight men who sleep with lots of women.

• Even if she could get two Straight men at a time, trying to get them into bed at the same time might be an issue. Straight men are not always comfortable with the idea of a 'threesome' where two of the partners are both 'male'. It may make them feel inadequate, or believe it to have 'gay' undertones. Even if it does happen, then it may get out of control as the two Yang energies start to compete against one another. So the woman may prefer to have her men 'one at a time' in order to get her Yang energy fix in a stable and controlled way.

I once knew several Straight men from the same rugby team, and they would boast continually about their sexual conquests, and about their latest four-some, six-some, or eight-some. However, when gently questioned... although all the men would be in the same room and constantly looking around at what their mates were doing... none of them ever felt comfortable about being in the same bed as their mates when they were with the lucky women. That would have just been 'too Gay'.

So it is indeed possible, and there are some Tantric women who actually seek out multiple, male sexual partners as way of 'harvesting' Yang energy (just as some Tantric men seek to harvest Yin from multiple women, regardless of whether these men are interested in the their partner's spiritual development or not).[3]

Within traditional Taoism, along with the acupuncture, herbs and Qi-Gong, there are also many formulas which are designed to cure illness through the correct application of sexual energies... and some sexual positions are meant to be beneficial for curing specific medical conditions.

---

3   You can read up more about these Straight Female practices in *The Sexual Teachings of the White Tigress: Secrets of the Female Taoist Masters* by Hsi Li.

Now, I am not arguing that modern medicine starts offering sex with Straight men to women with 'stuck energy' as a health treatment… as we shall see, there are other sources of Yang which are available and much easier to tap into… and probably far more reliable than some Straight men I know.[4]

If you can't find lots of men, then find one… but make sure that one man is really, really good at what he does. For more insight read *Beyond Tantra: Healing Through Taoist Sacred Sex* by Mieke and Stephen Wik. It's about a couple where the husband used Taoist Sexology to cure his wife of her medical condition (and they had fun while they were doing it)… See, I am not making this stuff up you know. It's all out there.

---

4   The other problem with getting sex on the British N.H.S. is that, financial budgets are under so much pressure, you could never be sure who they will prescribe for you, or what they might look like.

C13. Energy Polarity Type 2 - Straight Male & Straight Male:

In the 2nd Energy Polarity Type which we are going to explore, we put together two Straight Males, which means the Khat and Ka of both individuals are Yang in polarity. This is 4 units of Yang, the most you can get. What happens when there is such an extreme of Yang energy?

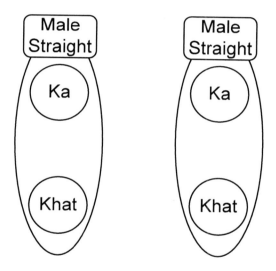

Figure 24: Straight Male to Straight Male

Well, what we find when you put two Straight Males together is that there is absolutely no attraction on *any* level, which means there is *no* flow of chi between them. In fact, the situation is to the contrary, there is only 'repulsion' on all levels, and this helps to account for a lot of things.

This polarity set-up means:

- Between each individual, the two Khats are pushing each other away (*horizontal*).

- Between each individual, the two Kas are pushing each other away (*horizontal*).

- Between each individual, the opposing Khat and Ka are pushing each other away (*diagonal*).

- Within each individual, their own Khat and Ka are also pushing each other away (*vertical*).

When we look at it from this perspective, it is complete and total repulsion on all levels... almost like an explosion of Yang.

Now, it would be wrong to say that all Straight Men are like 'rutting bulls'. Remember, we are describing core energies here, and how they are expressed will be different from individual to individual, depending on that individual's personality, culture, and upbringing, and also the ratio of Yin / Yang being expressed through their unique psyche / personality. Any man who has a high level of Yin within their personality will find this helps to tone down this overall explosion of Yang.

Although, it is interesting to note what happens when you put such a high Yin Male in the middle of a bunch of Yang Alpha Males, all of whom are competing with each other for 'top dog' status. The Yin Male will either flounder and be perceived as weak by the others... or he will be adopted / protected by a Yang Male who understands his 'value' to them, i.e. he helps them to switch off, recharge and find balance... which can give them a competitive advantage over all the others if they know how to use it / him correctly.

However, when we broaden our perspective to the collective, these core energies cannot help but underlie social and cultural interactions, and so, in general, Straight Men will be more aggressive, more assertive, and more combative in their relations with other Straight men... and so also to the world around them. Generally, this is bad news for Mother Earth, who over the last two centuries has borne the brunt of Yang Male aggression and competitiveness.

But what is really interesting about this particular polarity scenario... and this is the big problem with being your average heterosexual male... is that, the more aggressive a Straight Male is towards other Straight Males, the more aggressive he will also be to himself 'internally'. Remember, his physical Khat is Yang, and so he will be aggressive towards his own inner Ka, which is also Yang, and vice versa. This is probably why generally and collectively men are more sceptical about the existence of an inner world (i.e. If I can't touch it, it doesn't exist), and more standoffish of their own feelings. Because of the internal forces stacked against them, they find it much harder to *go within*.

There are three insights which we can draw from this particular energy set-up. For our first insight, we are quoting a section from Mathew Fox's excellent book *The Hidden Spirituality of Men*, where he is discussing one young man's discovery of his own spiritual nature:

> *This confession from a young man who is a science and business major is most revealing – and also scary. How many other young men have never connected with a spiritual side they do not know exists within them? ... How deeply have our schools and our religions truly failed us? ... One of the best kept secrets of our culture is that many men are deeply spiritual and care deeply about their spiritual life. It is a secret, however, because it is hidden – sometimes, as above, even from the men themselves.*[1]

---

1   Mathew Fox, page xi.

In contrast to the other polarity types for a Straight Men to connect internally, to discover their inner nature and spirituality is a bit like a salmon swimming upstream. Not impossible, but very, very tiring and exhausting… and at the end of it, society doesn't award you a medal, like it would if you had just set an Olympic record for the marathon. Such victories tend to remain quiet affairs, known only to the participants.

For our second observation, let us return to Paul Ekman's description of the Anga tribe of Papua New Guinea, who are unusual for their practice of homosexuality as the tribal 'norm', Straight men playing at being homosexual. The tribe is also known for being particularly aggressive and…

> … *Explosive in their anger, highly suspicious if not paranoid in character, and homosexual. It was the Anga that he was describing. His account fit with what we had been told by Gajdusek, who had worked with them. They had repeatedly attacked Australian officials who tried to maintain a government station there. They were known by their neighbours for their fierce suspiciousness. And the men led homosexual lives until the time of marriage. A few years later the ethologist Irenäus Eibl-Eibersfeldt literally had to run for his life when he attempted to work with them.*[2]

Other facts we can add to this picture of the Anga is that:

• Young men sexually 'service' the tribal elders in big communal huts.

• The tribe has a reputation for frequent and violent raids on neighbouring tribes.

Now, I once read a Gay writer who made the observation that if you

2   Paul Ekman, page 6.

ever wanted to see what male society would be like without the influence of women then just visit a 1970s Gay bathhouse.

I would argue that if you ever want to see what a totally male dominated society was like then visit the Anga (although, I wouldn't want to be a member of that tribe, and I certainly wouldn't want to live next door to them).

Although, in recent years, with the coming of the tourist dollar to Papua New Guinea, the Anga have toned down some of their fierceness, as they have realised that, in general, killing tourists isn't good for business.

Initially, people concluded that their extreme behaviour was due to their practice of homosexuality at the tribal level.

However, if we dig a little deeper then we find:

> • The Victorians used to believe that if male homosexuality was permitted then it would lead to the decline and ruin of Western civilisation. But their belief was that it would *feminise* men, but from what we have seen in Ancient Greece, and now with the Anga tribe, the opposite is indeed the case. It appears to make men more macho, more aggressive and more violent.

> • If Mother Nature does indeed only produce 3 to 10% true homosexuals in each generation, then it is not possible to ever create a population which is composed of 100% male homosexuals. This would mean that the Anga tribe is a minimum of 90% Straight males who, for whatever reason, engage in homosexual acts with their fellow tribesmen.

If we return to our polarity diagram for two Straight Males, given at the start of this section, this would lead to the creation of enormous amounts of competition, antagonism and aggression amongst the males... which will either destroy the tribe through internal conflict, or need to be safely released through projecting this aggression out onto 'outsiders'... i.e. raids on neighbouring villages, attacks on the government staff, and potential violence towards an intruding ethologist.

So the Victorians and the Chinese energy medicine practitioners were probably right, homosexuality is dangerous and harmful... *If practised by Straight Males...* because the 4 units of Yang generate too much latent aggression and violence.

But is it then also right to assume that it will be harmful for Gay Males as well... especially if the Yin / Yang polarity works differently for Gay Males?

The third observation is drawn from a recent documentary series entitled *Naked & Afraid.*

The premise of this show is that you take two American survivalists, one male and one female, remove their clothes and dump them in some inhospitable part of the planet... such as a desert, or jungle, or open savannah, or small mosquito infested island... and see if they can survive for 21 days alone, completely naked, with only their survival skills to help them.[3]

They were each allowed to bring one tool with them, and it was very interesting to see what each gender brought along.

For the women, the tool varied... it could be a cooking pot, or a saucepan, or a fire-starting kit... different, but always something practical. But for the men, it was always the same. They brought a knife. OK, sometimes it was a big knife, sometimes a machete, and sometimes it was more of an axe... but the boys always brought something sharp you would kill and cut with.

---

3   If you ever get to watch it, don't worry, this was a U.S. programme, and so all the private parts were pixelated out, so as not to offend its target audience.

That was the first thing which was very telling. But the programme also slowly revealed something else, which was really interesting about the difference between men and women, how they think, how they operate and how they approach life. I have to be careful here because your average man and woman does not sign up to spend 21 days naked in a desolate, dangerous and inhospitable part of the world (not unless they have something to prove, want to be noticed, have a deranged personality, or are trying to plug their latest survival book). The men and women on this programme were definitely not your average man and women in the street types.

But as the series unfolded, a recurring theme started to emerge which was very interesting and telling about how the genders think. Firstly, the women were much more *emotionally stable*, while the men were much more *emotionally bipolar*. The men would be emotionally up one minute, elated, triumphant and victorious (i.e. 'I am going to make this swamp my bitch!'), but then come crashing down to earth the next, especially if they had experienced a set-back. In contrast, the women appeared to be much better at coping with these set-backs, and so were able to hold it together both for themselves *and* their men.

This creates a picture of 100,000 years of human evolution, mostly in small tribes, where it was the women of the tribe who held things together, and ensured that their men didn't get to wound up and panicky. One of the tragic things about the continuing troubles in the Middle East is that because the role of women has been and is denigrated, and they are generally suppressed and and persecuted, women are unable to contain the energy of their menfolk, talk them down, and prevent them from doing stupid and violent things. The last 4,000 years of Middle Eastern history is an example of what happens when you leave the Straight men in charge.

So what was the point in having men... what positive element did, and do, the men bring? Well, it's a strange one... but if I had to put into words, men are much less prepared to put up with the status quo... which can be a good thing, or a bad thing, depending on circumstances, and the intelligence of the men involved. Overall, during the series, when the women had got to a place which was relatively stable, they would be happy with that, and would tend to stay there. But the men would be far less happy... and would grumble... and believe that things could be made *better*. They kept wondering if perhaps the grass was greener on the other side of the horizon... and maybe they should go and have a look.

Sometimes it was, sometimes it wasn't... but overall the men weren't prepared to make do, and would take risks to prove that they were right. In one episode, one man, tired of the fact they didn't have enough fresh water, drank directly from a small polluted stream... and would have died, if the film crew hadn't carted him off to hospital in time. But in another programme, another man, tired of the fact their camp kept getting flooded each night, persuaded his partner to go off on a risky hike to find higher land... which they eventually did, and were safe and dry for their remainder of their time in the swamp.

So over the last 100,000 years of human evolution, the women of the tribe have probably tried to talk their men out of doing something *stupid*, and tried to convince them to be happy with what they had got... Sometimes the women will have succeeded... but at other times, the men ignored them, and went off to do their stupid thing anyway (i.e. 'I'll show them...' being the classic thing men mutter under their breath when they turn their back on their partner).

Probably, half the time the men did something really stupid... like drinking contaminated water... killed themselves, and possibly their tribe... and so their culture and DNA wasn't passed on to the rest of humanity and the collective gene pool. The other half of the time, the men *did* discover something better... a better way to hunt, a better way to live... and the women had to reluctantly admit that their men had been right all along... and this new skill / knowledge was then passed down to subsequent generations... and humanity as a whole benefited.

Now, that is not to say that women can't initiate change, or that men can't exercise caution… But strange to say, that's what Straight Men appear to bring to the human party. From Evolution's perspective, Straight Men are the firecrackers which you throw into the middle of a party when it's getting too boring and you want to liven things up a little.

Up until recently, armies and the military were solely composed of male soldiers, and wars were fought by men. This is no longer the case. Women form part of the military in many Western countries, and have fought on the frontline, and in support, during several conflicts. However, there is still an ongoing debate as to whether or not this is good thing, and whether women have what it takes to fight and win in an actual battle. According to this theory, there isn't a definite yes or no answer to that debate, just that the inclusion of women makes things 'different'. The more Yin you add, the less Yang an army will become… which means if you need your army to be super-aggressive, as when Special Forces stormed the caves of Tora Bora in Afghanistan back in 2001, and were involved hand-to-hand combat, then this probably isn't a good thing. But, if you need a bit more Yin in your army to ensure it doesn't go off half-cocked, does think things through, and doesn't make stupid decisions the end up with more unnecessary deaths, then perhaps having a bit more Yin in the ranks might be a good thing after all.

C14. Energy Polarity Type 3 - Straight Female & Straight Female:

In the 3rd Energy Polarity Type which we are going to explore, we put together two Straight Females, which means both their Khats and Kas are Yin in polarity. 4 Yin units, which is the maximum Yin possible. What happens when there is such an extreme of Yin energy?

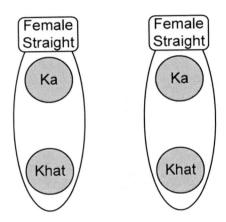

Figure 25: Female Straight to Straight Female

Well, when we put two Straight women together, there is absolutely no attraction at any level, so there is no energy flow. In fact, the situation is to the contrary, there is only 'repulsion' on all levels, and this helps to account for a lot of things. This polarity set-up means:

- The two Khat's are pushing each other away (*horizontal*).

- The two Ka's are pushing each other away (*horizontal*).

- For each individual, the opposing two Khats and Kas are pushing each other away (*diagonal*).

- Within each individual, their own Khat and Ka are also pushing each other away (*vertical*).

However, there is one fundamental difference to our last energy polarity type, the Straight Male, which is that within a Straight Female **Yin is not aggressive, it is not combative.** It yields and it holds, it supports and nurtures.

Once again we are referring to core energies, and an individual woman may not always conform to this image. However, generally, and in cultural and social interactions, women tend to be more supportive of each other, and more nurturing. In terms of this theory, their friendships will last longer then men's, and are generally much less combative and produce less friction.

This doesn't hold true for all women. If one individual woman has a lot of Yang energy in her personality, then she can climb to the top of the greasy management pole, and be just as 'bad ass' as any of the men. In fact, all the other women beneath her usually wonder why she isn't more supportive of the other females within the organisation, not realising that she just doesn't think like they do. And if two Straight Men have a good dose of Yin, they will also be able to manifest and maintain long-term, nurturing and supportive relationships as well as any woman. Remember, it's not about the gender, but about the percentage ratio of Yin / Yang within each individual. But she is not the norm, she is the exception. The majority of women are not like that.

There is something which I read once that said the nature of Yin is that which nurtures and nourishes, if you give 'something' to Yin it will nurture it and allow it to grow, to expand, and then give it back to you increased tenfold. This is true of the seed placed into the soil, and it is true of the baby growing within the mother's womb. This is why the womb and the earth are seen as being quintessentially Yin. But for Yin to do its thing takes time, it is not something which can be rushed. It takes around 9 months to make a baby, and around 9 months to make a new summer.

This is also true within the emotional arena. If a man gives a woman *love*, then she will take that love, nurture it, and give it back to her man tenfold. But if a man gives a women *hate*, then she will take that hate, nurture it, and give it back to her man tenfold... and you can't always predict when she is going to blow-up like a volcano... but she will, given time.

All women, but Straight Woman in particular, are the emotional incubators within any human society. If you abuse the women in your society, then you will not have a healthy or well-balanced society. Overall, a society reflects the way in which its women are treated, not just by the men, but also by the women themselves. One of the tricks in relationship counselling, to turn around a failing relationship, is to get the couple to focus on the things that first attracted them to one another, to those qualities they originally loved in their partner and not on all the issues and problems which are currently tearing them apart. If you can do that then you can change the whole dynamic between a man and a woman, so that the man is feeding the woman positive vibes and not negative, and she starts to feel good about herself. So although there is a total lack of Yang in this particular energy polarity set-up, there is also a great possibility for nurturing and support whenever a group of women come together.

However, there are a few other points we need to consider in this section, because it is not all Eve and the Garden of Eden here:

> • A friend of mine, who is involved with many complementary therapies, which tend to be run by women, has observed that if you have all women on the committee which runs the organisation then, despite the abundance of support and co-operation, things do tend to stagnate after a while, whereas

if you have at least one man on the committee then things tend to run more effectively... because you have at least one individual who can 'stir things up' when needed. Although, she also believes you need to have the right sort of man involved, someone who is in it for the right reasons, and not someone who likes being the centre of attention for all those women. The other option is to have a woman with a strong Yang mind. One of the biggest surprises of my life was the realisation that some men go on spiritual courses, not because they are genuinely interested in the subject, but because they find it a good way to meet single, unattached women. And, because they are usually the only man on the course, they don't have to deal with any potential competition from other rutting stags.

• There is one recent period in history when the demographic balance between the sexes was seriously thrown off balance, the decades after World War 1. During this war, so many men were slaughtered in the trenches, so many potential husbands and boyfriends never made it back to their loved ones that after the war there was a serious lack of men to go around... and sadly many unscrupulous men took advantage of this fact, and many, many women were forced to live out the remainder of their lives unfulfilled and 'single'. There are stories from the 1920s of parties where 30 plus women were all competing for the attentions of one single, eligible man (who didn't have to be that good looking to draw their attention)... and remember, Yin doesn't like to compete, it's not aggressive.

There is also a story of a headmistress at one English female boarding school, gently informing her soon to be graduating sixth-form class, that the world into which they were about to emerge was not the one they were brought up to expect. Many of them wouldn't be able to find suitable young men to marry and have a family with, there just weren't enough young men left to go around, and so they would have to find happiness in 'other ways'.

When I was much younger, I once knew a couple of 'heterosexual' spinster ladies who, because of World War 1, had entered into a quiet Gay partnership as a way of finding happiness (although the true nature of their relationship was never mentioned in polite society). Now, from my young perspective, I always felt that their happiness was tinged with a degree of sadness. It seemed to me that they had found a way of being happy, but in an ideal world, it is not what they would have 'preferred'. But it was preferable to a life of loneliness, or heartbreak at the hands of some unscrupulous Casanova.

Strangely, I think this is actually one of the main differences between Yin and Yang, especially when it is expressed through the human genders. The majority of the time Yin knows that it needs Yang to achieve its full potential, to be truly fulfilled. However, in contrast, Yang often foolishly believes it can go it alone, and doesn't need Yin, and this can cause no end of pain and problems. Yang can waste a lifetime searching for 'perfection', whereas Yin is prepared to be pragmatic, and settle down with a workable, if not perfect, solution. Also if the situation had been reversed, if millions of women had suddenly died out overnight, I seriously doubt that Straight Men would have come up with similar practical arrangements. OK, a few practically minded ones would have. But the majority of Straight Men would have probably started another war over the few females still remaining.[1]

• When writing this chapter, the idea crept into my head that if this theory is indeed correct then it will be reflected in the difference between riots in male and female prisons. Because of the super surplus of Yang energy, male prisoners should be more likely to riot than female prisoners, who should be more

1   More information about this can be found in Virginia Nicholson's book *Singled Out: How Two Million Women Survived Without Men After The First World War* (Viking, 2008).

Yin and so less aggressive. In fact, I could recollect several famous male prison riots, but not a single riot within a female prison. However, when I did do some research on the Internet it soon became clear that riots in female prisons do occur (i.e. Kingston, Ontario 1994) but such incidents are much *rarer* then the male variety, and so maybe the exception. I am not saying that a female prison is a nice place to be, and I believe female prisoners are more likely to have a big dose of Yang, which is why they are not your average female. But overall, there is less likely to be a build of volcanic Yang in a female prison.

• In his book *The Secret of Secrets*, a discourse on the Taoist classic *The Secret of the Golden Flower*, the mystic Osho makes the point that Yin creates society, Yin builds civilisation. If it was left to Yang, then there would be no society, no civilisation... the human race would still be in small hunter-gatherer communities, roaming across the landscape, and living in tents. In a similar way, it is usually the Matriarch which holds a family together, along with the relationships between the females of the family (i.e. it is the female who remembers to send a birthday card, arranges the family gatherings, and generally keeps the family connections alive). This is not to say that Patriarchs and male members don't have a positive role to play as well (i.e. mowing the lawn, cleaning the car, getting a round of drinks in)... but Yang is not the holding and stabilising force, Yin is. In fact, human civilisation and the first human cities probably started when one or more women said, 'I'm tired of trekking all over the tundra, following the migrating herds, watching you men get all macho with your spears and arrows. Why don't we stay right *here*, and instead *grow* our own food? Would that be too much to ask? And you can start by building me a proper toilet which is more than just a smelly hole in the ground.'

• As we saw in the last chapter, Yin is more emotionally stable compared to Yang, while Yang is more likely to jump into action then Yin. This means that the relationship between two Straight

Females is bound to be more emotionally stable and supportive, although also more risk adverse then between two Straight Males.

• For the last 3,000 to 4,000 years human civilisation has been a patriarchy, ruled by kings and other dominant men / priests. However, there is strong evidence to suggest, previous to that, human civilisation was much more of a matriarchy, with powerful women in charge, and the people worshipped the Great Goddess. When the Aryans swept down from the Northern steppes around 1500 B.C, it is believed that they swept away the last traces of these matriarchal societies and cultures, replacing the Great Goddess with worship of the Sky Gods.

I once got into trouble on a personal development course, with a group of women who were adamant that society needed to return to the old ways, to the ways of the ancient matriarchy, as it was 3,500 years ago. As the lone male in the group, I was holding the line that, as there is so little known about this time, we can't just assume that it was any better than *now*... and why is a society ruled by women any better than a society ruled by men? Surely, the best thing is to find a balance between the two, between Yin and Yang?

To say any of this was apparently sacrilege against the 'old ways', and I was lucky to get out of that room with my life.

But I still believe it is the truth, a matriarchal society is probably no better than a patriarchal society. If the human race is to mature then it needs to find a way forward which balances the two extremes. An extreme patriarchal society is too unstable and chaotic, but an extreme matriarchal society is too resistant to change, and so tends to stagnate. Right now in human history, we are at stage in our development where we can afford neither of these two alternatives.

Now, I can quote two interesting pieces of history to support my case here. The first comes from the history of the Iroquois tribe of Native America, where all the important decisions were taken by a council of women. Now you would expect this to have been a more stable, and peaceful society. However, that was not the case. This council of female elders was constantly sending the male warriors off to do battle with neighbouring tribes, especially if they felt their land had been invaded, or their pride hurt. In fact, the male warriors once complained that the women, having no experience of war, sent young men off to die far too easily, not understanding the consequences of their decisions.

The seconds comes from the 1970s and 80s, and involves the 20th Century mystic we touched on earlier, Osho. He preached that much of the problems with modern society was due to the suppression of female energies, and things wouldn't get better until there was a rebalancing between the sexes. To achieve this, and Osho wasn't afraid to put his money where his mouth was, he put women in charge of all his ashrams and meditation centres around the world. In the early 1980s, Osho moved from his ashram in India to a large ranch in Wasco County, Oregon, U.S.A., known as Rajneeshpuram. In 1985, the female in charge of this commune, known as Sheela, along with 20 other top officials, mainly female sannyasins, were found guilty of attempted murder, wiretapping, bugging, poisoning, and arson.

This proves that even when the women are put in charge, doesn't mean that they cannot behave just as badly as the men... and I seriously doubt that there ever was a matriarchal utopia 4,000 years ago, where everything was perfect and just. I believe that the answer isn't to keep see-sawing from one polarity to the other... the answer is to find a balance point between the two, a balance point between Yin and Yang. But we can only achieve that if our society learns to understand, respect and integrate Yin energy.

C15. Energy Polarity Type 4 - Gay Male & Gay Male:

In the 4th Energy Polarity Type which we are going to explore, we put together two Gay Males, which means both their Khats and Kas are opposite in polarity. This gives 2 Yang and 2 Yin, a 50 / 50 split. What happens in this kind of relationship?

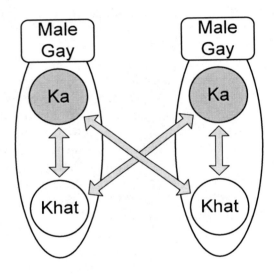

Figure 26: Gay Male to Gay Male

Well, when we put together two Gay males, then several interesting things occur. On the *negative* side:

> • The Khats are the same polarity, are repulsive, and because they are Yang they could be hostile / aggressive towards each other (*horizontal*).

- The Kas are also the same polarity, repulsive, but because they are Yin will not be as aggressive (*horizontal*).

But on the *positive* side:

- There is a polarity flow occurring within each individual, as the Khat is Yang and the Ka is Yin. This means that a Gay man has an internal polarity which he can use for 'solo cultivation' if he were to choose. A Gay man is therefore more open to their inner world, to their spiritual nature, compared to a Straight Male, because they are not continually pushing it away, there is no repulsion between their Khat and Ka (*vertical*).

- There is a polarity between each Khat and the opposing Ka on either side. So the more the Gay couple can open up to their energy bodies, their Kas, the more stable and fulfilling their relationship can become (*diagonal*).

This picture also supports the traditional Native American belief that a Gay person is 'two souled', that they have within their natures both male and female energies, and so have a broader perspective on the human condition. So once again, we have formed a Figure Eight shape, just as we did with the Straight Couple, but this time it is *lying on its side*.

This creates a difference between a Straight and Gay couple, especially if they want the relationship to deepen and be successful. For the Straight relationship to be successful, each partner needs to draw upon the Yin or Yang of their partner. However, for a Gay Male relationship to be successful and stable, each partner needs to draw upon the Yin energy within their own energy field, and then later upon the Yin energy of their partner's Ka. When the Gay couple can achieve this, then their shared energy can flow throughout the entire Figure 8.

So the good news is that, according to GPT, there is a polarity flow amongst all 4 units... so we have the achieved a solid foundation for a viable form of Gay Tantra. OK, it's a different shape to the Straight couple, but that doesn't mean it is not as *stable*, and because the energy can flow easily between Yin and Yang, then there is the potential for *expansion*. However, this type of relationship is a game of 'two halves' and this helps explain a few of the common preconceptions about Gay men which exist within our society.

As I said earlier, I once read a Gay writer make the observation that if you ever wanted to see what male society would be like without the influence of women then just visit a 1970s Gay bathhouse. And this is one of the main preconceptions which many Straight people have of Gay men... that they are sex mad and are keen to avoid a committed relationship... and this is indeed true of some Gay men... but then this can also be laid at the door of many heterosexual men as well, because both share a Yang Khat.

However, I once read an article by a right-wing journalist who was arguing that Gay men should not be allowed to adopt kids because their relationships do not last, are inherently unstable, and when they eventually break-up then any kids they had adopted would suffer emotionally and mentally. Now, as much as I would like to violently disagree with this woman, the theory points to the fact that two Yang Khats are not predisposed towards having a stable and long-term relationship... and that is true if the Yang Khats belong to either Straight or Gay males. Two Yang Khats are predisposed towards aggression and conflict, which is true whether the couple are Straight or Gay, unless they are able to draw upon a source of Yin to balance things out, because it is Yin which brings stability and commitment into any relationship.

If the Straight male is able to draw upon the Yin of a loving woman then he should be able to calm down and enter into a committed, long-term relationship (unique personality traits not withstanding). And if a Gay male is able to draw upon the Yin of their own Ka then they can also slow things down and enter into a committed, long-term relationship... and the key to being able to do that is *self-love* and *self-worth*. If the Gay male(s) are able to love themselves, then they can easily access their Ka, even when they are not even conscious of doing so and this changes the nature and potential of their relationships. If two Gay men are able to access and draw upon the Yin energy radiating from their respective Kas... then the whole dynamic of their relationship will change, and they are just as capable of manifesting a loving, long-term and committed relationship as any Straight couple on the planet (and there is no reason why they cannot adopt as well, because their relationship will be just as stable as any heterosexual partnership).

I once read an article, which was based on a survey of children in authority care, awaiting adoption. Obviously, the older the child becomes, the harder it is to find couples willing to adopt them. Asked if they minded whether any potential adoptive parents were Straight or Gay, the majority of the kids replied that they didn't care about the sexuality of their adoptive parents, they just wanted to find a stable home, with a loving and supportive set of parents. Once again, the need to love, be loved, and find a nurturing emotional connection with other human beings is more important than morality and prejudice. And if they can do this, then Gay men are able to draw upon one of the advantages in their particular energetic set-up.

You see, initially Straight men go to great lengths trying to win themselves a female partner, but once she is won, once they have plugged into, or married, a source of external Yin, then a Straight male often sits back and sits on their laurels. Why change and grow when they have already won the 'main prize'. While the wife remains by his side, the Straight man doesn't need to worry about losing her Yin energy... and he may even give up on trying to keep the relationship 'alive'.

But for a Gay man, the Yin energy which he is plugging into is not external to himself, it originates from his own Ka, and so there is less chance for him, and any Gay relationship he has entered into, from 'stagnating'... just as long as he can keep his own inner polarity flowing. So if a Gay man, or Gay men within a relationship, has been able to connect with their Ka(s) then their energy will be much more flowing and dynamic overall.

Over time, loving Straight couples always say that the initial burning lust turns into love, and 2-Dimensional sex transforms into 3-Dimensional 'making love', and may even turn spiritual, which is also possible if you bring Yin into the energy mix, because Yin holds, transforms and deepens the sexual energy. I believe that the same potential exists for Gay men, sex can also transform into love, but this also requires that the Gay men reach up and connect with their Yin Kas... which is not that hard for Gay men to do, and also offers them a route to develop a spiritual side to their sexuality.

Because for a Gay man, the polarity between their Khat and Ka is not repulsive (Yang / Yang) as it is for a Straight man, it is attractive (Yang / Yin). Gay men therefore have a natural disposition towards inner transformation, because their internal Khat and Ka is naturally attracted to one another. This means that, even when a Gay man is not in an external relationship, they can still be in an internal relationship with their own Ka, they can still exchange love and energy with their Ka, and so they can still achieve a sense of inner fulfilment. As I said earlier, Gay men will find 'solo cultivation' much easier than Straight men will.

But then the question becomes, 'Why haven't more Gay men stumbled upon this potential before?' And my answer to that question is three words... culture, religion and society... which we can wrap up into one simple sentence...

More Gay men would probably discover this for themselves if they didn't have to also deal with the total crap which their society, culture and religion tries to dump on them from the start of their life.

I believe that many Gay men do feel the pull of their inner polarity early on in their lives, but because their society, culture or religion believes their type of sexuality to be unnatural, sinful, or abhorrent... they desperately try to push it away... and so frustrate and hinder what should be a simple and beautiful process. It's really a question of an inner pull versus an external pull.

The person in front of them, their father, mother or priest is a physical reality... but the inclinations within them are only inner feelings. It is always easier for a child to suppress their inner feelings then do battle with external authority figures, especially when every child wants and needs to 'fit in' to survive. If you think of it from the perspective of a young Christian man growing up in England during the 1950s, where the authorities used to practice chemical castration or aversion therapy if they caught male homosexuals... or in modern day Iran, where the punishment upon being captured is public execution (plus whatever else they do to you in prison before the day of your execution)... then is it any wonder that men in such circumstances try to hide who they are, repress their inner feelings, try to lead a quiet life, do what their family and society expects of them, get married, settle down, and have kids.

There is series of books by the author Philip Pullman, known as the *His Dark Materials* trilogy, set in a parallel universe where, from the moment of birth, children are constantly accompanied by daemons, the animal embodiments of their inner-selves. The Magisterium, a powerful religious organisation that represses heresy, develops a process which can severe the etheric link between a child and its daemon, although this always results in a virtual lobotomy for the child involved. However, that's a small price to pay, because this process will give the Magisterium greater power and control over the human populace of their world. When I consider all the different ways in which medicine and the Church has tried to 'cure' homosexuals over the centuries, I cannot help but think of the Magisterium trying to pass a knife between a Gay Man's Khat and Ka, even though this may result in cutting off part of his Soul in the process. They would argue that they are doing this to save his Soul... but I don't believe a word of it. I doubt they even know what a Soul is, let alone what it feels like to have one.

On the surface, there is nothing which might betray the secret of their hearts. But on the inside, no matter how good they have been at repressing and suppressing their true feelings and nature, there will be moments when a quiet voice whispers to them of a different kind of life... of what might have been, if they could have faced their fears, or lived in a different kind of world. Alongside this voice there is the constant guilt and shame about whom and what they are... and a constant questioning, 'What did I ever do to deserve this? Why did God make me this way? Why was the Devil allowed to corrupt me while I was in the womb?'

For such unfortunate Gay Men, there is no one they can talk to, as this would run the danger of exposing themselves and their secret... no one they can turn to, no one they can trust to make sense of it all... there is only a heart crushing sense of loneliness and self-hate (which also has to be hidden from the people around them, because if you let out one secret, all the rest might come tumbling out as well). Is it any wonder then that many men in such circumstances conduct a mental lobotomy on themselves, desperate to cut out the part of them which, they believe, has ruined their lives?

As you were reading that last section, how did it make you feel... fearful, sad, angry, or disempowered? Well, that's how they *want* you to feel... They want Gay men to feel like there is no hope... that's what their power is ultimately based on... depriving others of positive feelings... depriving others of their birth right. It's sad and sick, but true.

But there is also good news. In certain parts of the world, there are now countries and areas where this is no longer the case, where Gay Men do not have to think like that, and no longer have to act like that. According to the theory, Gay Men should never see themselves as being less or deprived internally, because that is just not the case. Gay Men are different, and although that difference does close some doors on an energy level, it also opens others... and the possibility of Gay spirituality is to be found through one of those doors. For Gay Males, this polarity scenario is the foundation upon which Gay Polarity Tantra is built.

Remember the name the traditional Native Americans used to describe homosexuals... they said they were 'two-souled'.

If Gay Men do indeed have 'two souls' within them, then their path to true happiness can only be found through allowing these two souls to express their love for one another internally, and also their love for other Gay Men externally, men who have a similar multiple occupancy of the heart.

C16. Energy Polarity Type 5 - Gay Female & Gay Female:

In the 5th Energy Polarity Type which we are going to explore, we put together a Gay Female and a Gay Female, which means their two Khats are the same polarity, and their two Kas are also of the same polarity... and it is their Khat and Ka which are internally opposed. This gives us 2 Yang units and 2 Yin units. What happens in this kind of relationship?

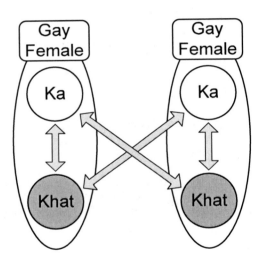

Figure 27: Gay Female to Gay Female

On the *negative* side:

• The two Khats are the same polarity, are therefore repulsive, but because they are Yin they will not be hostile / aggressive towards each other (*horizontal*).

- The two Kas are the same polarity, are therefore repulsive, and because they are Yang they may be hostile / aggressive towards each other (*horizontal*).

But on the *positive* side:

- There is an energy flow between the two Gay Khats and Kas, which makes each women potentially more emotionally stable (*vertical*).

- There is an energy flow between each Woman's Ka and Khat (*diagonal*).

Just as with Gay Men, here between two Gay Women we also see the Figure Eight shape on its side, which means that all 4 units are connected and included, providing the maximum level of fulfillment for each individual.

For Gay Females, this is the foundation upon which Gay Polarity Tantra is built, as it is the most connected and beneficial structure from the perspective of energy flow. Admittedly, there may be too much Yin on the physical level, which could lead to a stuckness in the relationship, and too much Yang on the higher level, which could lead to aggression... but if the two women are able to enter into a deeper energy partnership, and form the relevant connections, the mixture of the Yin and Yang from both levels will help to balance things out, and lead to a deeper level of love, support and beneficial expression.

C17. Energy Polarity Type 6 - Straight Male & Gay Male:

In the 6th Energy Polarity Type which we are going to explore, we put together a Straight Male and a Gay Male, which means their two Khats are of the same polarity, but their two Kas are opposite in polarity. This gives us 3 Yang units and 1 Yin unit. What happens in this kind of relationship?

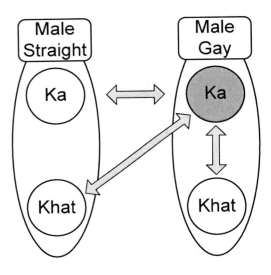

Figure 28: Gay Male to Straight Male

Obviously, there is much more Yang in this set-up then Yin, and the only Yin available is the Gay man's Ka.

On the *negative* side:

- The two Khats are the same polarity, are therefore repulsive, and because they are Yang they could be hostile / aggressive towards each other (*horizontal*).

- The Straight Male's Khat and Kas are also of the same polarity, and so repulsive. In fact, they should be able to generate far more 'internal' aggression and hostility then the Gay Male (*diagonal*).

But on the *positive* side:

- There is an energy flow between the Gay Man's Khat and Ka, which makes him potentially more emotionally stable (*vertical*).

- There is an energy flow between the Gay Man's Ka and the Straight Man's Khat (*diagonal*).

- There is an energy flow between the two Kas, Gay and Straight (*horizontal*).

As we have previously said, because the Straight Man's Khat and Ka are of the same polarity, they will be naturally antagonistic towards each other, and it is also highly likely that this aggression / tension will be projected out on to any external individual they come into contact or relationship with. Remember, the Straight Male is the most emotionally unstable of all the polarity types, and so more prone to projection than to psychological ownership.

Unfortunately, this is what tends to happen when Straight Men come into contact with Gay Men. Historically, it could be argued that Straight Men have been more aggressive towards, and been more persecuting of, Gay men more than they have of Gay women.

Why might this be? Well, obviously there is more aggressive Yang in this kind of relationship, and so there is more aggression moving around, waiting for some target to fix on too... and there isn't enough Yin to calm things down.

But, according to the theory, the surprising thing is that the Straight Male is also attracted to the Gay Male... or at least to his Yin Ka, and for most Straight Males this is all taking place on the unconscious or semi-conscious level. As you can see in the diagram, not only is the Straight Khat attracted to the Gay Ka, but the Straight Ka is also attracted to the Gay Ka. The Straight Khat will either be oblivious to the attraction between the two Kas, or if it has some vague sense of it, because the Straight Khat and Straight Ka are antagonistic towards each other, because of their internal repulsion, the Straight Khat may feel rivalry over this competing energy connection.

Now, if the Straight Man's personality has achieved a certain degree of ego-integration, is mature and grounded, when they experience any passing sexual feeling towards another man, which does reach into their consciousness, it won't throw them off balance. They will acknowledge it, but then decide not to act on it.

Like one mature, middle-aged Straight Male once said to me, 'Yes, I have experienced these kinds of feelings occasionally... but I have never wanted to follow them up, because they don't interest me.' However, at the other extreme, this also explains why some Straight Males *do* have homosexual dalliances when younger (usually in their teens), exploring their sexuality, but then decide to settle down in a conventional Straight, heterosexual relationship. Many people assume that these men must be either Gay or Bisexual, but I don't believe this is always the case. I believe that they do experience a real sexual attraction, explore it, but then decide that it's not for them, because it is not as fulfilling... especially when you consider that this kind of relationship doesn't contain sufficient Yin to ground and stabilise their Yang. In fact, these kinds of relationships would be highly instable, and so eventually blow up or burn themselves out.[1] However, these two possibilities require that the Straight Male is *comfortable* with these sexual feelings when they arise, and also with

---

1   As we shall see in a later chapter, there are a few potential energy benefits for a Straight Male in such a relationship with a Gay Male.

themselves.[2]

But what happens when they arise within someone who is uncomfortable with the whole idea and practise of homosexuality, or is paranoid or fearful about the possibility of being perceived as Gay, or has been raised in a society in which homosexuals are actively reviled and persecuted (or all three)? Under these circumstances, what happens when the Straight Khat experiences an unconscious or conscious attraction to a Gay Man's Ka? Well, I believe that what happens in such circumstances is that:

a) They choose to reject and suppress these unwanted and reviled feelings;

b) They project all the hate and revulsion they feel onto the unfortunate Gay Man who has unexpectedly stirred up these feelings.

Because there is so much explosive Yang in this relationship, so much latent aggression, what we have here is a mixture of buried attractions and open aggression, which can so easily turn to persecution and violence. Remember, your average Straight Male is the most emotionally unstable of all the 4 polarity types, and because they are so Yang, they often act without stopping to think things through.

Usually, it is presumed that these aggressive Males are all trying to hide their own homosexuality by projecting it on to those who are, as a way to hide their own true nature (i.e. they are persecuting homosexuals because they are themselves closet homosexuals).

This may be true for some cases. However, the theory suggests that it is more likely to be Straight Males, experiencing a burst of sexual attraction towards an unfortunate Gay Man, and going on the offensive as a way of disowning these unwanted feelings. Either way, it is the poor Gay Male who suffers the violence and the onslaught

2   We'll be exploring the Bisexual Polarity set-up in another chapter.

from the Straight Male who isn't able to 'shrug off' this unexpected and unwanted 'attraction'. Across the planet, Straight Men routinely commit violent acts against Gay Men:

- There was a news story about Islamic State members throwing an unfortunate Gay Man off the roof of a building, and then as he lay dying on the ground, they stoned what was left of him... just to be on the safe side.

- During 2005, in Iran, two young men, believed to be 16 and 17, who were caught engaging in homosexual acts, were strung up together, side by side, in a public execution. The photo taken, with the young men with cloth hoods on their heads, just before the stools are kicked out from underneath their feet, is available to view on the Internet. An Iranian minister is on record telling British MPs that homosexuals should be tortured and killed. Why torture? Why is it so important to this Iranian minister that he inflict severe pain on Gay Men... unless there is something else going on inside that man's head?

- The Russian Federation has passed legislation against homosexuality, and many heterosexual vigilantes, who may be under the guidance of the authorities, use this as an excuse for attacking Gays without impunity.

- Even in the 'enlightened' United States, there are many stories of Gay high school students being attacked and murdered by their straight school mates, apparently for just being 'different'.

These stories are the ones which have managed to hit the world's news headlines. How many other Gay Men suffer terribly, all alone, in the dark, and we never hear about them or their plight. There are many African states where homosexuality is outlawed, and atrocities probably take place quietly within their prisons. Out of sight, out of mind.

I feel that *Leviticus* Chapters 18 and 20 have a lot to answer for. Leviticus 18: 'You shall not lie with a male as with a woman; it is an abomination.' Leviticus 20 'If a man lies with a male as with a woman, both of them have committed an abomination; they shall surely be put to death; their blood is upon them.' In other words, we're going to kill you and it is all your fault. However, the Bible doesn't mention any prohibition against Lesbian behaviour... although religious fanatics and fundamentalists are 'prepared to read between God's lines' and use Leviticus 18 and 20 to condemn Gay Women as well.

Now, I am not arguing that every Straight man is really Gay, and just won't own up to it. That's not it at all... I believe that's often a fantasy put about by some Gay Men to ease their feelings of alienation. Instead, what I am saying – because the theory is pointing in that direction – is that there is a polarity and attraction between Gay and Straight Men which complicates their relationship, and which can lead to acceptance or violence, usually depending on the psychological maturity of the Straight Man involved. Also these attractions often don't make conscious sense to the Straight Man, because he isn't supposed to be attracted to the Gay man's Khat standing in front of him, because they are both Yang and so repulsive / aggressive. He's attracted to the Gay Man's Ka, something he can't see.[3]

As we have said, if the Straight Man has been brought up in a culture which doesn't have a problem with homosexuality, then when / if these 'attractions' did start to arise on the edge of their consciousness, then the Straight man will probably brush them aside, and not take them as a sign of mental instability or evil. And because there is no real attraction between the two Khats, only repulsion, these feelings won't be acted upon (because it usually takes 'all four to tango'). However, if the Straight Man has been brought up in a culture which actively persecutes homosexuals, and these same feelings start to surface in someone who hates the very idea, even if only in the corners of

---

3   Because of this, I seriously doubt that Straight Men ever get turned on by Gay porn. There has to be a real person / Ka involved for the polarity to work its 'magic'.

their mind, then the Straight Man will become aggressive, project their hate on to the 'other', and try and destroy the Gay Man who is the focus of their attraction. Their unconscious hope is that if they destroy the 'other', the hated homosexual, then they will also destroy those same, uncomfortable, evil feelings within them. And this is exactly what will happen, as the Straight Man won't have anyone else to have a polarity relationship with... until the next Gay Man comes along... and the next, and the next. But your average fundamentalist is quite prepared to murder and kill a hundred, or a thousand, or even a billion if it wins them their place in heaven.

If the Gay Man had more Yin, then he might be able to contain and balance the situation, but what Yin he does have is at the Ka level, and so not directly available to the Khat.

Important: Actually, there is a Polarity Aikido which a Gay man can do which may help to deal with these aggressive situations, but more on that in a later section, when we explore the question of energy boundaries from the Gay perspective.

But now... let's end this chapter with a more uplifting thought. Back in the 1930s and 40s, the gifted psychic Edgar Cayce, who was also known as 'the Sleeping Prophet', and who was also a committed Christian, used his gifts to help people who were suffering from physical illness and mental distress. Over time, as he saw more and more people helped by his psychic readings, he slowly learnt to be more flexible about how you 'interpret' the Bible.

During one of these readings, a man, who was 'suffering' from his homosexual feelings, asked for a personal reading to explain why God had cursed him which his 'condition', and how he could be cured. Edgar Cayce's guide tuned into the young man's aura and explained that, during a previous lifetime in 16th Century France, he had been a nobleman who had ridiculed and persecuted many homosexuals, and because of this negative karmic debt, he had reincarnated as a homosexual in this lifetime so that he could repay his karmic debt, and learn acceptance for his 'condition'. What's also interesting about this story is that, as a young man, Edgar Cayce started out as a dedicated Christian, who had read the entire Bible several times over, and probably treated every word of Leviticus as 'gospel'. So if Cayce's guide was just an expression of his unconscious mind then you might have expected him to sit in severe judgement over any homosexuals he was reading for. But this is not the case... his guide did not talk about condemnation and damnation, but about forgiveness and acceptance.

Now, one lesson which you might take from this story is that if you have incarnated as Gay in this lifetime it may be due to that fact that you persecuted homosexuals in a previous lifetime... and this may be true for some people (especially those who throw Gay men off roofs and then stone them to death). It may be true for a few... but not the majority. Because there is another much more positive view which I take from this young man's story and the response of Edgar Cayce's guide.

If God really does hate homosexuals, as Leviticus 18 and 20 suggests, then this young man wouldn't have been sent back in this lifetime to learn acceptance and forgiveness for homosexuals and homosexuality. In fact, if that interpretation was correct God should have given him a medal, not turn him into another homosexual. But God, or the Tao, or Great Spirit... or whatever Divine force you choose to believe in, *didn't do that*. His punishment for his past-life crimes was to be sent back to try and learn acceptance for his condition... which suggests to me that God doesn't really have a problem with homosexuals, but with anger, hate and the evil which is done in His / Her name. It's the Straight Men who write, and then later interpret, the scriptures who have the problem.

In this real story, the punishment wasn't directed at the homosexuals, it was directed at the one who persecuted the homosexuals... who showed hate and intolerance, and not love and acceptance. It appears *those* are the things which God really cares about, not whether 'a man lies with a male as with a woman'. And that is the God I choose to believe in...

And as Gandalf the Grey says in *The Lord of the Rings: Fellowship of the Ring*, that is 'a much more optimistic thought entirely'.

C18. Energy Polarity Type 7 - Straight Female & Gay Female:

In the 7th Energy Polarity Type which we are going to explore, we put together a Straight Female and a Gay Female, which means their two Khats are of the same polarity, but their two Kas are opposite in polarity. This gives us 3 Yang units and 1 Yin unit. What happens in this kind of relationship?

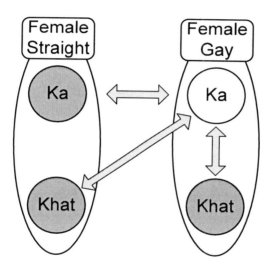

Figure 29: Gay Female to Straight Female

Obviously, there is much more Yin in this set-up then Yang, and the only Yang available is the Gay Woman's Ka.

On the *negative* side:

- The two Khats are the same polarity, are therefore repulsive, but because they are Yin they will be less hostile / aggressive towards each other (*horizontal*).

• The Straight Female's Khat and Ka are also of the same polarity, and so repulsive, although not aggressively so (*diagonal*).

But on the *positive* side:

• There is an energy flow between the Gay Woman's Khat and Ka, which makes her potentially more emotionally stable (*vertical*).

• There is an energy flow between the Gay Woman's Ka and the Straight Woman's Khat (*diagonal*).

• There is an energy flow between the two Kas, Gay and Straight (*horizontal*).

Now, there is a story, and I am not sure how historically accurate it is, that when Queen Victoria was presented with the official bill to sign which would make homosexuality illegal within the United Kingdom, she refused to sign the part which would outlaw female homosexuality. Not because she was an enlighened monarch ahead of her time.. But because she couldn't imagine that women would 'do that sort of thing'. But women do *do* that sort of thing... and on the whole, Straight Females are more open minded accepting of their Gay sisters then Straight Males are of Gay Males.

Why? Well, I think there are three reasons for this:

• Overall, Yin is less aggressive, and so less likely to venture down the road of persecution than is Yang. This means that, even when a Straight Woman is not attracted to other Females, she is less likely to want to attack or persecute them. This isn't the Yin way.

• Even though it is not on the physical level, from Khat to Khat,

Straight Women are still attracted to the Yang Ka of a Gay Woman, and it is the kind of attraction which would not be so threatening to either party. Generally, I believe that Straight Women are less inclided to be freaked out by any such attraction.

• Because there is quite a lot of Yin in this type of relationship, both women are far more likely to keep things 'grounded' and in 'perspective', and not allow any negative emotions to run amok.

• The spark of Yang within the Gay Woman's Ka will be attractive to the Straight Woman, and therefore it may even be beneficial for her to be in some kind of relationship with the Gay Woman, especially if she does not have any other source of Yang.

Now, if we look back to Chapter 14, and recall the shortage of male partners after World War 1, then we can see that a Straight Woman settling down and forming a loving and sexual partnership with a Gay Woman would not be wholly implausible, and I am sure that it happened more than once during this period. We also need to remember that polygamy between a man and multiple wives has never been on offer within the Church of England, so that route was not available.

For a Straight Woman after World War 1, unable to find themselves a husband, a Gay / Straight relationship may have been preferable to the two available alternatives:

• A life of spinsterhood

• A relationship with a married man (a series of one night stands, or brief, passing liasons)

Interestingly, in this particular Energy Polarity type all 4 units are connected up in some way and, although it is not a perfect fit, at least it is better than nothing, and women are more able to make a Gay

/ Straight relationship work successfully than men, because there is more containing and nurturing Yin available, and less expansive and aggressive Yang.

But the Gay Khat is not connected energetically to any unit in the Straight Female, and so will be the unit that will feel the most left out and excluded. So over the long-term, the Gay Female may find the relationship less fulfilling than the Straight Woman, although the abundance of Yin available in this type of relationship will probably help to hold them together in a loving and supportive partnership.

C19. Energy Polarity Type 8 - Straight Female & Gay Male:

In the 8th Energy Polarity Type which we are going to explore, we put together a Gay Male and a Straight Female, which means their two Khats are of the opposite polarity, but their two Kas are of the same polarity. This gives us 1 Yang units and 3 Yin units. What happens in this kind of relationship?

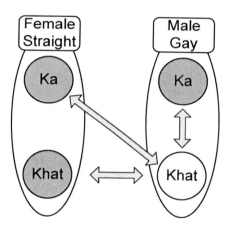

Figure 30: Gay Male to Straight Female

On the *negative* side:

• The two Kas are the same polarity, are therefore repulsive, but because they are Yin they will not be hostile / aggressive towards each other (*horizontal*).

• The Gay Female's Khat and Kas are of same polarity, but because they are Yin are less likely to be aggressive and hostile to each other (*diagonal*).

There is no attraction or energy flow between the Gay Male Ka and the Straight Female Ka (*horizontal*).

But on the *positive* side:

  • There is an energy flow between the Gay Man's Khat and Ka, which makes him potentially more emotionally stable (*vertical*).

  • There is an energy flow between the Gay Man's Khat and the Straight Woman's Ka (*diagonal*).

  • There is an energy flow between the two Khats, Gay and Straight (*horizontal*).

This is one of those Energy Polarity Types which isn't perfect, and yet is better than some of the others, and if Gay Man wanted to hide who they were in a hostile Straight society, this would be one of the situations which would allow them to do it.

All 4 units are connected up, although the Gay Man's Ka is not connected to anything on the Straight Woman's side, and so is likely to be the unit which feels the most unfulfilled.

Up until exploring this Energy Polarity type, I had always assumed that Gay Men marry Straight Woman because they are trying to hide their sexuality, and there must have been an element of this in many marriages down through the centuries.

I had always assumed that:

  • The Gay Man must be consciously aware of what they are doing but chose to go down this route for various reasons, most often because they have no other socially acceptable choice.

- The Gay Man must be in continual *inner pain*, and faking it to make the relationship work.

For many Gay Men born into countries and cultures were homosexuality is reviled, outlawed and persecuted, I am sure this is often the case.

But now I am not so sure that is *always* the case. True, for many societies and cultures, a Gay Man must hide their sexuality in order to avoid persecution, even death. But when you look at the diagram which accompanies this Energy Polarity type you can't help but see an attraction between the two Khats, and so there is the potential for love and attraction within this kind of relationship, and it is an attraction which exists on the physical. This means it is possible for love and sexual attraction to exist between a Gay Man and Straight Woman.

Therefore, I freely admit that I was wrong to assume that this kind of relationship is just about the Gay Man *hiding*. These relationships do indeed have the potential to blossom and deepen into something more. The amount of Yin, on both sides, would mean it would be a very stable kind of relationship, although the Gay Male might find it a little boring and stifling over time, and may be inclined to escape and have the odd, occassonal fling. In fact, overall, it is more likely that the Straight Woman will get more of her energy needs met then the Gay Man will, due to the more energy connections which are available to her.

Because the Gay Man's Ka is the one who is energetically shut out of this type of relationship, this could generate feelings of unease, and require the occasional adventure to keep the Gay Ka happy if the Gay Man cannot supress this side of them... or at least an escape into a lustful fantasy.

A lot will depend on the social and cultural circumstances within which the Gay Man finds himself, and the levels of honesty and trust between both partners. If the Straight Woman doesn't know that her husband is Gay before the marriage, and then finds out in unfavourable circumstances, then there is likely to be hell to pay, as Yin is not prone to forgive and forget easily. Yin definitely knows how to hold and harbour a grudge. But overall, it's not the worst Energy Polarity possible, and these two individuals, given favourable circumstances, just might lucky enouth to live a happy and fulfilled life together.

C20. Energy Polarity Type 9 - Straight Male & Gay Female:

In the 9th Energy Polarity Type which we are going to explore, we put together a Straight Male and a Gay Female, which means their two Khats are of the opposite polarity, but their two Kas are of the same polarity. This gives us 3 Yang units and 1 Yin unit. What happens in this kind of relationship?

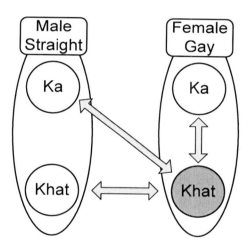

Figure 31: Straight Male to Gay Female

On the *negative* side:

- The two Kas are the same polarity, are therefore repulsive, and because they are Yang they will also generate a hostile / aggressive energy towards each other (*horizontal*).

- The Straight Male's Khat and Kas are of same polarity, and will also generate a repulsive and aggressive energy (*diagonal*).

• There is no attraction or energy flow between the Straight Male Ka and the Gay Female Ka (*horizontal*).

But on the *positive* side:

• There is an energy flow between the Gay Female's Khat and Ka, which makes her potentially more emotionally stable (*vertical*).

• There is an energy flow between the Straight Man's Khat and the Gay Woman's Ka (*diagonal*).

• There is an energy flow and attraction between the two Khat, Gay and Straight (*horizontal*).

Back in the early 1990s, I was completing an M.A. at a University in the North of England, and sharing a house with a number of other mature students. One day a letter arrived, addressed to one of the students who had lived in the house the year before, and since we had no forwarding address, and no other way to contact her, the envelope sat on the mantlepiece for a week or so, until the young woman working on a Phd. in Astrophysics decided to open it. It was from a Straight young man, in response to a personal advert which the female student had placed in Gay Times, looking for a Lesbian lover. In his reply to her advert, the Straight Man admitted that he wasn't a Gay Woman, but he would be grateful if he could be allowed to be in the room and watch while she had sex with her lovers... and if he might be allowed to join in, well, that would be his idea of total heaven.

What does this story tells us? It tells us that many Straight Men are totally fascinated by Gay Women.

Which when you look at the Energy Polarity diagram for this type of set-up, actually makes sense. In this type of relationship, each of the

4 units are included in some way, and so it is so energetically viable relationship, and one which may be a way for a Gay women to survive in a hostile culture and society.

There are two strong attraction lines between a Gay Female and a Straight Male, although the Male is likely to get more out of the relationship then the Gay Female will, and we also need to realise that once again her Gay Ka is effectively locked out of any energetic connection with the Straight Male, and so may feel excluded and unfulfilled over time. But the problem this type of relationship is the amount of Yang, especially stored up behind the scenes.

It is probably this surplus of Yang which excites a Straight Man and turns him on. However, it is also this excess of Yang which would also make this kind of relationship volatile, aggressive, and unstable. So on the physical level, between the two Khats, love and attraction is possible, although it is a relationship which might have to weather the storms of internal conflict and even rivalry between these two partners.

C21. Energy Polarity Type 10 - Gay Male & Gay Female:

In the 10th and final Energy Polarity Type which we are going to explore, we put together a Gay Male and a Gay Female, which means their two Khats are of the opposite polarity, but their two Kas are also opposite in polarity. This gives us 2 Yang units and 2 Yin units. What happens in this kind of relationship?

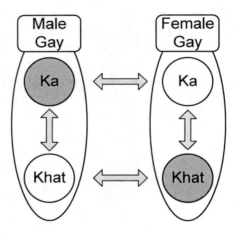

Figure 32: Gay Male to Gay Female

On the *negative* side:

> • These is no connection across from either Khat to the opposing Ka (*diagona*).

But on the *positive* side:

> • There is an energy flow between the Gay Man's Khat and Ka,

which makes him potentially more emotionally stable, and the same is also true for the Gay Woman (*vertical*).

• There is an energy flow between the Gay Man's Khat and the Gay Woman's Khat (*diagonal*).

• There is also an energy flow between the two Gay Kas (*diagonal*).

Common sense would suggest that this Energy Polarity type should not work... and yet is does. When you also look at the alternatives, if a Gay Man or Woman cannot find a partner of their sexual persuasion and type, then it appears that their next best option is to find a Gay individual of the opposite gender.

In times past, this was probably the best way to survive in challenging and unsupportive times, and the great thing was that this kind of relationship does not preclude love developing between both individuals. For example, back in the first part of the 20th Century, the writer Vita SackvilleWest was married to the historian Harold Nicholson, and they had two sons, Nigel and Benedict. However, what the rest of society didn't see was that Vita was a lesbian, having relationships with such notable women as Virginia Wolf, and that Harold was gay, and there was an 'open marriage', which was able to accomodate their many and varied tastes. And yet, they both loved and cared for each other, by all acounts had a stable marriage, and even discussed their extra-curicular affairs and dalliances with one another.

Now I am not saying that every Gay Man should link up with a Gay Woman. I believe that there is something important about developing the diagonal energy lines between the Gay Khats and Kas, which are not included in this Energy Polarity Type. But over the centuries and millenia, I would not be surprised to discover that many people considered themselves fortunate to find themseves in this kind of relationship.

C22. Circling the Square:

There is a belief that human beings learn all the important stuff while in relationship with another human being.

- It starts when we are a small baby, learning about self-love and our emotions through our relationship with our mother, which hopefully equips us for life with a grounded and well-adjusted personality.

- Later, we learn about our culture and society through our social interactions with our friends and family.

- We learn practical information from the relationships with our teachers, whether formal or informal, which hopefully gives us all the intellectual and practical skills we will need to navigate our way through life.

- We learn about deep and true love through a relationship with our *significant other*, and according to Attachment Theory, we all have a deep-seated, primal need for an emotional connection to at least one other human being, and when that connection is either under threat, or has become severed completely, we can behave in stupid and irrational ways, trying to re-establish this emotional connection once again.

- Finally, throughout our lives other people reflect back to us the unresolved issues which lurk within our unconscious mind, usually through the psychological phenomenon of 'projection'.

When we are deprieved of any of these relationships then we cannot grow into our true potential, fit in with the rest of society, or uncover who we truly are.

Now if relationships are so important, understanding the energetic, archetypal forces which underpin these relationships is probably essential if we want to ever understand what is really going on beneath the surface. That is why I have spent time going through each of the 10 Energy Polarity Types in turn.

However, before we move on, there are two things which I need to clarify.

One:

Interesting story. I was once employed by an I.T. company which decided to outsource a large section of its I.T. department to India for financial reasons. This meant that a group of Indian project managers analysts, developers and testers came over the U.K. to learn about the company's products and services so that they could successfully take this knowledge back with them to the Indian sub-continent. The whole thing was a total disaster, badly managed by the 'impatient' English senior managers, and the company almost went bankrupt as a result, and the Indian office was eventually closed down... but that is another story for another time.

This particular story involves how many of the male Indian I.T. workers went online to find their future wives. You see, I got to know several of them quite well during this transition period, and one day they showed me the Indian equivalent of a 'dating website'. Basically, if you were a young man, who didn't trust your mother and grandmother to arrange the right sort of wedding for you, you could visit this particular website and find your own professional bride, which was apparently quite revolutionary and shocking at the time.

But there were three things which I found very interesting:

- It was usually the women posting themselves online, seldom the men. Obviously, in Indian culture, it was seen as demeaning for the men to advertise themselves in that way, unless they were really desperate to find a wife.

• It was essential for the man to have a qualification which was *equal to* or *higher than* their wife, and if a women had a higher qualification then she was immediately perceived as *undesirable*. For example, if the man had a Ph.D then he would be happy to marry a woman with a simple B.A. or B.Sc. But a man with a B.A. would not feel comfortable, or consider marrying a woman who already had an M.A., M.Sc., or Ph.D. This meant that all the women who had foolishly gone on to complete their Ph.Ds could only expect to marry a man with an equal qualification.

• But what I found most interesting, through listening to the Indian I.T., workers, was that love and physical appearance, although important, was not their primary concern. It was almost as if they were about to enter into a financial or business arrangement, that would provide the basis for their future prosperity, the raising of their children... and hopefully love, mutual respect, and sexual attraction would also appear over time. But at the start of their search, love and sexual attraction wasn't their primary concern, finding a suitable 'professional' match was.

In the Western world, we generally believe that the best relationships are formed when individuals are sexually attracted to one another, mutual love and respect develops, and finally the couple decide to spend the rest of their lives together because of *love* and an *emotional connection*.

However, this is not the primary concern of many different societies and cultures around the world... and it has not always been the primary conern within Europe either. In fact, the concept of marriage for love is a relatively recent development in our social history. Before then, marriage was more about formalising an alliance between two families, a way to ensure the families wealth and power was managed and passed down through the generations. Such a marriage *might* lead to love and respect between the partners, but this was not always the case.

In fact, the concept of romantic love only really took hold around the time of the Middle Ages, popularised by the concept of courtly love and the songs of wandering troubadours in Europe during the 12th and 13th Centuries. It wasn't until the 13th Century that the Catholic church was able to impose the concept of formal marriage on the good citizens of Europe who, up until that point, had confirmed their marriage contract 'under a tree, in a tavern, or in a bed' without the presence or blessing of a Catholic priest.

So the first clarification I am making here is that each individual views relationships through the prism of their own beliefs and cultural conditioning, and so the the polarity of Yin & Yang, whether working through the *individual* or *archetypal levels*, is also being expressed and filtered through that larger social and cultural context.

Two:

In the previous chapters, I may have given the impression that Gay Men come in for serious persecution, while Gay Women get off more lightly in terms of social and cultural condemnation.

Although at the *archetypal level*, it is true that Yin is non-aggressive, and so Gay Woman often has less negativity and aggression to deal with, when we move up to the *individual level*, and look at the world around us, Gay Women often come in for the same amount of aggression and hostility from their community as do Gay Men.

Recently in the U.K. on Channel 4 there was a documentary about teenagers growing up as openly Gay. This documentary clearly showed the level of persecution which some Gay teenagers had to deal with from their families, schoolmates, community, and society...

even through the simple act of walking down the street and *not* trying to hide who and what they were, being out and proud, could bring forth hostility. Compared to my own teenage years, these Gay teenagers also had to contend with Internet trolls and cyber-bullying. Even when they closed the door to the own home, and should have been safe and secure, just switching on their mobile phone or computer meant the cyber-bullies could still pour poison into their heads through Facebook or Twitter accounts. And this was happening to Gay males *and* Gay females.

I have also seen this fact reflected in documentraies on the trans-gender community in the U.S. where people were being actively persecuted and bullied regardless of whether they expressed themselves as male or female.

Bottomline, it's tough out there for many people, regardless of whether you are Gay male, female, or trans-gender, and regardless of what the *archetypal level* might suggest, Gay Women can come in for as much hostility as Gay Men. Tragic, but true.

Now, compared to the people above, so far in my life I have had it pretty easy. I grew up in rural Devon, and although the kids in my fifth and sixth-forms all knew I was gay, I never received any hassles because of it. I suppose I was lucky.

The only time I can ever recall receiving open hostility was while I was studying for my degree in London, and someone cut the brakes on my bike. The college was situated on top of a hill, and there was a busy road at the bottom of the hill, a junction where you always had to stop and wait for a safe break in the traffic before proceeding. If I had realised too late that someone had cut the brakes, I would not have been able to stop myself in time, come speeding down the hill and out into the oncoming traffic, and so might have ended up underneath a passing lorry or bus... and you wouldn't be reading this book now. Fortunately, I realised that both brakes had been cut early on in the journey, and before I had got to the dangerous junction...

and so walked all the way home, pushing my now 'castrated' bike along with me.

Who did it? Well, I had no hard proof... but in my own mind I believe it was the friends of a sports jock who had recently left the college under a 'dark cloud', and who I knew was struggling with their own sexuality. His homophobic friends must have been upset that he had been forced out by the college authorities, and decided to take it out on me, although I had done nothng to deserve it... and I also have a vague memory of seeing them lingering around my bike. But this all happened 30 plus years ago now, and nothing like that has happened to me since... and since then I have come out to my parents, family, and close friends... and my life has never been rocked to the core by anyone's open rejection. I suppose I have been lucky.

But the point I would like to end this chapter on is that no theory can predict everything that can or will happen to everyone, and a lot depends on the social and cultural context in which we find ourselves, the connections which are created between ourselves and other people, and what happens to be going on inside the heads of those other people (especially the haters, the fanatics and the bigots).

If I had grown up in Iran or Saudi Arabia, my life would have been very, very different. I would have had to hide who I was... and I would have never been able to access the information which has supported my spiritual path to date. But I didn't, I was born in the U.K. and raised in rural Devon, with the right kind of information, people and relationships around me to support me on life's journey. And I am so very grateful for that fact.

C23. What About the Bisexuals?:

At the end of the popular 1960s children's cartoon series *Scooby Doo*, there was always a scene where that episode's ghost or monster was unmasked, thus revealing that they were only just an ordinary man or woman underneath the disguise.

This scene was no doubt included to inform all the children watching at home a) not to be scared because it wasn't real; b) there is always a logical explanation to explain what happens in life; and c) there is no such thing as ghosts and the supernatural, just a bad man in a mask. I am sure that that particular scene was inserted at the insistence of the studio execs to ensure American kids didn't get the wrong ideas from the show. However, in the 21st Century, with TV shows such as *Buffy the Vampire Slayer*, *Supernatural*, and *The Vampire Diaries*, studio execs don't seem to have those same kinds of concerns.

During this scene, the villain uttered those now famous lines, 'And I would have got away with too if it hadn't been for you pesky kids!' For a while I harboured similar feelings... *Because the theory of Gay Polarity Tantra would be perfect if it wasn't for those pesky bisexuals!*

Let me explain. According to Wikipedia, bisexuality is defined as:

> ... *romantic attraction, sexual attraction or sexual behaviour toward both males and females, and may also encompass romantic or sexual attraction to people of any gender identity or to a person irrespective of that person's biological sex or gender, which is sometimes termed pansexuality.*
>
> *The term bisexuality is mainly used in the context of human attraction to denote romantic or sexual feelings toward both men and women, and the concept is one*

of the three main classifications of sexual orientation along with heterosexuality and homosexuality, which are each parts of the heterosexual-homosexual continuum. A bisexual identity does not necessarily equate to equal sexual attraction to both sexes; commonly, people who have a distinct but not exclusive sexual preference for one sex over the other also identify themselves as bisexual.

Also, according to Wikipedia, *the heterosexual-homosexual continuum* 'is a psychological and philosophical understanding of human sexuality that places sexual orientation on a continuous spectrum from heterosexuality to homosexuality, with sexuality ranging from exclusive attraction to the opposite sex to exclusive attraction to the same sex.'

This is a similar idea to the one I have been exploring in this book, where sexual expression isn't a single either / or affair, but is actually a much broader and more complex expression of the Yin / Yang polarity, a spectrum along which an individual can identify or place themselves in one of several different positions... or even shift about between different positions, as the mood takes them.

Bisexuals are therefore individuals, either men or women, who are not only sexually attracted to members of the *opposite sex*, they are also happy and comfortable with the idea and reality of having sexual interaction with someone of the *same sex* as themselves, regardless of whether that other person defines themselves as being Straight or Gay. It is wrong to say that bisexuals will get into bed with anyone... but their sexuality is much more fluid and flowing, and so can be much harder to pin down. This is why they find it easier to hide in amongst a crowd, and can play it Straight when they need to.

Now for a long time I didn't understand how bisexuals fitted into the theory which we have been exploring in this book, nor did I have sufficient practical experience of working with bisexuals to understand how their energy expressed itself. For a while, I actually thought the theory might be incomplete in some way, or needed to be amended to incorporate bisexuals... although I couldn't see how to amend it.

But then I had a breakthrough moment, an *epiphany*... I realised I didn't need to change or amend the theory, because the theory was perfectly OK as it was. All I needed to do was change how I perceived bisexuals in relation to the theory.

Remember what I wrote earlier, that bisexuals are happy and comfortable with the idea and reality of having sex with either sex / gender? That was the missing key... and the clue was the words *happy* and *comfortable*. Bisexuals don't have a problem with exploring their sexuality, exploring their polarity type, whereas Straight and Gay individuals often do.

The theory we have been exploring in this book is built upon 10 energy polarity scenarios, which explore the energy set-up between Straight Men, Straight Woman, Gay Men and Gay Women. These then are the four cornerstones of *the heterosexual-homosexual continuum*.

But one of the things we saw through our exploration of each of the 10 energy polarities earlier was that attraction could potentially occur in the most unlikely places, between a Straight Man and a Gay Man say, or a Straight Woman and a Gay Woman. It wasn't always the best fit, but if there was a spark of attraction then it could be acted upon... but only if the individuals were willing and comfortable with the idea.

The epiphany occurred when I realised that bisexuality isn't about energy polarity, it's much more about individual *personality*. As Richard Thornton wrote earlier about the Cherokee, they 'believed that having attraction to both men and women was normal, although not characteristic of all Cherokees.' This means it is perfectly normal for a Straight Man to be attracted to a Gay Man, or a Straight Woman to a Gay Woman... but it is not characteristic of all Straight individuals. It's possible... but not necessarily the norm, and it is up to the individual as to whether they want to act upon it.

Therefore, you can have a bisexual Straight Male, who is comfortable with having sex with a Gay Man, Straight Woman, Straight Man, or Gay Woman... and you could also have a bisexual Gay Man who is also comfortable with having sex with the same list of potential partners. If there is a Yin / Yang exchange going on between the parties involved, then attraction is possible.

Basically, bisexuals have personalities which are more open to exploring the true potential contained within their sexuality.

I am therefore proposing that bisexuality isn't a distinct energy polarity type, but a personality type which is comfortable with exploring all the possible connections which their polarity type can make. If it is a personality type then family upbringing, society and culture will also play a heavy role in this. I don't believe there are going to be many bisexuals in Iran, because why would you run the risk of a death sentence when it is far easier to keep playing it Straight? And so the theory does not need to be amended, it already supports this possibility and points towards a conclusion.

Also, when we re-read the quote from Wikipedia at the start of this chapter, we find that it states 'A bisexual identity does not necessarily equate to equal sexual attraction to both sexes; commonly, people who have a distinct but not exclusive sexual preference for one sex over the other also identify themselves as bisexual.' Not all types of sexual attraction are equal, but for a bisexual, some are more equal than others... think about it.

Therefore, it is perfectly natural to have bisexuals who play the field, but who primarily identify as a Straight Male, and who will eventually settle down with a Straight Woman and raise a family. But it is also equally possible to have bisexuals who play the field, but who choose instead to identify as a Gay Male, and will eventually choose to settle down with a Gay Male partner... because that is the polarity which they find the most fulfilling. (And there will also be those who never choose to settle down, whether Straight or Gay, because as individuals that is what they prefer.) Ditto Straight Females and Gay Females... although in the millennia before the 21st Century, they would have found these lifestyle choices harder to implement, and still do in fundamentalist countries.

Remember, although many of the scenarios show that polarity can be established, and energy can flow between the two partners, there is only one where the maximum benefit and result is achieved, where all 4 units are engaged... and it is towards those scenarios that I believe all the polarity types eventually gravitate, because it is the most fulfilling for them. And I believe that is the one towards which the majority of bisexuals gravitate towards in the end... after they have explored all the other options available to them, because that is the one which they find the most *fulfilling*... whether Straight or Gay.

Most human beings aren't stupid and will eventually work out, via trial and error, what is best for them as individuals in the end... as long as there isn't a priest or preacher filling their heads with nonsense ideas and so leading them down the wrong track. That is how I currently believe that bisexuals fit into the existing Gay Polarity theory. It's not that bisexuals were being awkward, just that I didn't really understand how they functioned... which, in the end, comes down to the fact they are much more comfortable with their own sexuality, whatever that might be, then your average Straight or Gay individual.

C24. Energy Boundaries for Gay People:

Now the eagle eyed among you may have noticed a discrepancy in our previous Energy Polarity types, or at least a potential which I didn't explore in any great detail.

I made the statement that Polarity Scenario 4 was the foundation for Tantra for Gay Men, and Polarity Scenario 5 was the foundation for Tantra for Gay Women, because these are the two scenarios where all 4 units are included, and a Figure 8 pattern is created which maximises the flow of energy amongst all of those 4 units. But these are *not* the only scenarios where energy flow is created.

In Polarity Scenario 6 an energy flow is created between a Gay Man and a Straight Man, and in Polarity Scenario 7 an energy flow is created between a Gay Woman and a Straight Woman. Both of these routes are indeed possible, and they have a workable polarity... and some people have established loving and fulfiling relationships based on these poalrity types.

For a Gay Male / Straight Male, there is no polarity flow possible between the two Khats, but there is between the two Kas, and also there is a diagonal flow occurring between the Gay Ka and the Straight Khat. The horizontal connection between the Gay Male's Khat and Ka is also in existence. The same is also true for the Gay Female / Straight Female scenario, although the polarity of the Khats and Kas are obviously reversed.

OK, not the best scenarios available, but there is an energy flow occurring. There is no Figure Eight in these scenarios, but at least 4 of the 3 units are included, and there are two lines connecting the two individuals.

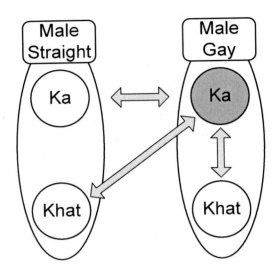

Figure 33: Energy Polarity Scenario 6

Based on this, I can already hear someone out there in Reader land saying, 'Doesn't that mean I could possibly win over that Straight Guy / Girl I have always fancied? OK, our relationship wouldn't be connecting up all 4 units, but I could put up with that... It's better than *nothing*.'

Yes, you are quite correct. The theory does indeed say that such a relationship is possible... but is it *really* better than nothing? Are you 100% sure about that?

You see, in the practical energy side of Gay Polarity Tantra, I will *not* be showing you how to go about creating those kinds of energy connection, or making available the vibrational techniques which could create and support those energy connections.

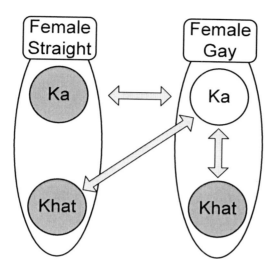

Figure 34: Energy Polarity Scenario 7

I know I am being a killjoy, and ruining your dreams of a happy ever after with Straight Thomas or Tabitha, or whatever their name might be… but I am doing this for your own good. Trust me, been there, I know what I am talking about here. These pathways offer false hope, but ultimately lead nowhere which is real or fulfilling.

Firstly, if you look at the two diagrams above you will see that, even though energy connections are created, and 3 units are included, *the unit which is always excluded in each of these scenarios is the Gay Khat.*

This means *you*, the physical personality, *you* the person who is reading this now.

This means that if this type of relationship were ever to become a reality, you would be forever excluded from the circulating energy and love between the other 3 units.

Unfortunately, the bottom-line is... *there is absolutely nothing in it for **you***.

So if there really is nothing positive in this kind of relationship for you... the question is why would you ever consider it? Why would you ever give it the time of day? Well, the answer to that question is also to be found in the two diagrams. Because the second thing we notice is that, although you, the Khat is getting nothing from this relationship, your focus on the Straight 'other' is of great benefit to your Gay Ka. Of all the units involved, this is the one which is getting the maximum energy flow, from both the Straight Khat and Straight Ka.

Although you the Gay Khat isn't benefiting from this kind of relationship, your Gay Ka is loving it... and remember, the strongest kind of attraction is diagonal. Even though the Gay Khat is getting no positive benefit, there is still a tremendous magnetic attraction being created from the Gay Ka level towards the Straight individual, which is why the Gay Khat finds it so hard to break away, and move on and find a real relationship which is more supportive, because the Gay Ka wants to keep the relationship intact.

When this kind of situation manifests the Gay individual finds that that their Khat and Ka are pulling in opposite directions. The Khat wants to break free, while the Ka wants to maintain the attraction. In fact, in these sort of 'relationships' the attraction is only being generated from the Gay Ka, and if you take this out of the equation then you would be left with two Yang Khats (Gay and Straight) which would be pushing each other away.

Unfortunately, because energy is also flowing internally between the Gay Khat and Gay Ka, the Khat feels the Kas attraction to the Straight person *as if* it were its own... which can get very confusing. Until, the Gay Khat can communicate with the Gay Ka, and re-educate /

re-orientate it away from this Straight 'addiction' then it will be very hard for the Gay Khat to break away, as it needs to be something they both agree on.

However, the third thing which this diagram is showing us is that the other beneficiaries of this particular set-up is the Straight individual, both Khat and Ka, who are on the receiving end of this flow of positive energy from the Gay Ka. Potentially, there is an attraction there, and although the Gay Khat cannot benefit from it, the Straight Khat and Ka *can* and *do*.

Now let's assume that the Straight Khat doesn't freak out over this, and try and persecute the Gay Male or Female... and that they are able to remain *comfortable* with this attraction, whether at a conscious or unconscious level. If the Straight Male is able to do this then they are in a win-win situation.

They probably don't want to jump into bed with their Gay friend, because there is no polarity / energy flow between them on the physical Khat level (although some might, just to see what the fuss is all about) on the archetypal level. But the Straight Male is getting energy back from the Gay Ka, and so from their point of view it makes sense to keep their Gay friend *hanging around*. It's a bit like someone giving you free money, and you don't need to do a single thing to earn it. Unfortunately, this can easily turn into a situation where the Gay friend hangs around the Straight friend, gets nothing concrete back in return, while the Straight friend gets to benefit from all the positive energy which they are receiving.

Now, it is important to realise that this isn't true for *all* Gay / Straight friendships. I believe it is only a small percentage of Straight people who come to rely on the energy hit from their Gay friend... and the majority of Straight people, who are comfortable with the energy set-up, do not abuse the energy relationship in this way. Besides, the Gay Ka isn't going to hook up with every Straight individual they meet... there are other factors at play.

But, unfortunately, there are those few who do, and flirt with Gay people as a way of opening up a source of Yin / Yang which they can use for their own ends. In this way, the Gay Male / Female can be seduced into continuing the relationship for years, because they are flattered by the attention, or are trapped by their fantasies, and hope that something will come of it eventually. This is why I do not, and will not be teaching how to activate the energy connections supporting these types of relationships. These paths are just too problematic, and can potentially open up a Gay individual to manipulation by an unscrupulous Straight individual.

Indeed, the opposite is the case. Instead of showing you how to open these energy routes up, I need to show you how to close them down! It is through these two routes that Gay people are open to manipulation by Straight people (not all of them, but some), and when you close them down, you start to see the truth about your relationship with this person... was it for real or manipulative? One potential clue to what is really happening between you both is to ask the question, 'Was my Straight friend's life working before they met me?' If the answer is 'No', they only started to be successful after they met you and became friends, then this is a good sign that they are riding upon your energy (and your Ka has become fixated on them).

The real test of your relationship is to energetically close down the route between your Ka and their Khat / Ka and see what happens next, see how you feel and how they react to the sudden absence of your energy. Remember, this dance is all happening on the unconscious level, and so they probably won't be able to express in words their feelings... but the relationship between you will start to change in big or subtle ways.

For example, I once realised that this was going on between myself and a Straight young man, who I had been mentoring and nurturing since the age of 18. Before I met him, his life was a bit of a 'car crash' and going in completely the wrong direction, and I helped him to get on his feet, stabilise his life, and encouraged him to embark on a successful career. His response was that I was 'brilliant' and we would be friends for life. However, eventually, I realised that I was also supporting him energetically, which is not in my own best interests, and so I closed down the energy connection, and the result was he simply 'drifted off'... and I haven't seen or heard from him for years.

Now, in this particular relationship, I was not consciously viewing this Straight young man as a potential romantic partner, and so it was probably easier to spot what was going on and disconnect. However, if I had been unconsciously projecting on to him, and dreaming about our future together, then this would have made the whole situation harder to deal with, detect, and so more difficult to break free of.

But there are other variations upon this basic game which we need to be aware of. For example, as the above diagram shows, the same thing can happen between a Gay Male and Straight Female. This is especially true if the man in her life is totally non-existent, and so she looks to the Gay Man as an easy and convenient source of Yang. Or even, if she has a man, but her current male partner is inadequate or deficient in some way, she may look to her Gay male friends to fill the 'gap'. These kinds of relationship can become very close and very incestuous.

Once again, close the energy route down for a while, and observe how it impacts on your intimate relationship... and also see how it feels for you to keep 100% of your own energy. When I closed down one such dodgy energy connection between myself and a Straight Woman it resulted in my own life suddenly taking shape and surging forwards in the right direction. It was only when I closed down the connection that I realised how much I had been supporting her energetically. One of the results of disconnecting is the book you are reading now because I suddenly had more energy available to focus on the things which mattered to me.

The potential for energy manipulation is also there in a relationship between a Gay Female and Straight Female, in the same way we just explored, where the Straight female can view the Gay Female as a ready and convenient source of Yang. The Straight Female may draw upon the Gay Female's Yang energy as a way to supplement the lack of Yang in her own life.

Finally, the potential for energy manipulation is also there in a relationship between a Gay Female and Straight Male, in the same way as we discussed previously... as a ready source of Yin. The Straight Male may also draw upon the Gay Female's Yin energy as a way to supplement the lack of Yin in his own life. As I said a little earlier, these particular energy set-ups potentially exist in any relationship between Gay and Straight individuals... and not all of these relationships descend into some kind of *energy vampirism*, where the Straight individual is feeding off the Gay individual. In fact very few such relationships end up going down this route. But it *can* happen, and so you need to be vigilant.

The key to understanding the difference between those relationships that do and those that don't is simple. It is do with an individual's *energetic boundaries*. Yes, these attractions exist in any Gay / Straight relationship... but they cannot make the Gay individual lower their energetic boundary to the Straight person. That can only occur if the Gay person makes a conscious or unconscious decision to do so... and if they do that, then the Gay person is opening themselves to no end of pain, because they are allowing any unscrupulous person to ransack their energy.

But why would a Gay person want to lower their shields, and leave themselves unprotected? Basically, the same reason anyone does really. Low self-esteem, lack of self-worth, the desperate need to be loved and an emotional connection to someone else... all of these internal drives trick us into opening our energy field up to the wrong sort of person... because we foolishly believe that any kind of intimacy is better than none, and loneliness is such a killer of the heart.

Important: That last statement is 100% not true. Being intimate with Dracula will only leave you drained of all life-force. You should only lower your energy boundaries when in the presence of people who love and support you, and do not wish to manipulate you or your energy for their own gains. So if you find yourself in such an abusing relationship, what do you need to do practically to get yourself free of the person and situation?

Well, what I suggest is:

- You need to re-orientate your Ka so that it disconnects from the unscrupulous Straight person. There are several ways you can do this... but primarily, your best bet is to strengthen the horizontal connection between you and your Ka.

- You need to close down the energy connection between you and the Straight other, and any access which you have previously given them into your energy field.

The second one becomes a lot easier if you have previously completed the first one.

Now, as we shall soon discover, Kas need to be fed, and their food is love, ecstasy, any feeling which is positive, enhancing and uplifting.[1] These types of positive energies improve the health and wellbeing of the Ka, which in turn benefits the Khat. However, for the vast majority of the time, Kas get little or no attention from their Khats (especially the Straight ones).

Is it any wonder then that Kas are therefore inclined to flirt energetically with anyone who is prepared to show them a just little attention? From the Kas point of view, it isn't wrong... especially if they feel cut off and lonely.

---

1   Sexual orgasm is just the ticket for that... especially if it occurs within the context of a loving, nurturing relationship.

Unfortunately, as we have seen, these types of relationship are open to potential abuse, especially if a Straight Khat is unconsciously involved in the interaction. A Gay Ka having an energy relationship with a Straight Khat & Ka can work, because Kas are not limited by time / space / morality and culture in the same way Khats are. But once again, such a relationship it isn't fulfilling for the Gay Khat, because they are not included in the equation, and they will be continually forced to pursue something which is not obtainable… or even edible. In these types of energy relationship, it is the Gay person who usually comes off worst, whereas the Straight person has the best of both worlds.

These types of Ka connections also raise the problem of 'energy permission'. In energy healing, there is a rule that says you can only send healing energy to someone who has given their conscious permission to receive it. Normally, we are just asking energy permission of the Khat, the physical self. But if we conclude that the Ka has an independent consciousness then don't we also need its permission?

Alternatively, the Ka 'could' be making energy connections which its associated Khat is totally oblivious to, unaware of, and would not be happy about. If you see a good-looking Male / Female working down the road, what is to stop your Ka from making an energy connection to their Ka, without the permission of your Khat or theirs? Their Ka may be up for it, and may reply, 'Great, whatever has my Ka done for me?'

It gets a little complicated from this point onwards… and working out what is and is not ethical is a total headache. Although I am convinced Kas are also capable of saying 'No, thank you' if they are not interested in another Ka. And this is another reason why I don't believe it is a good ideas to put the 'how to do it' into the public domain. I mean every desirable Male / Female pop star and film star could potentially get their Kas hit, and it would be too much bad karma involved for me to contemplate.[2] So even though these routes are possible, they are problematic, and we will be sticking to the two 'positive' routes we described earlier (i.e. Polarity Scenario 4 and Polarity Scenario 5).

However, if you are a lonely Gay kid in Ohio or Nebraska, and you have worked with your Ka, found it responds, and you want to work with another Gay Ka, then there 'is a way'. Just for you, I haven't closed that route down in the energy journeys which I am creating. But you will need to discover it for yourself, using the information based in this book. I am not just going to hand it to you on a plate... so learn to think *outside the box*.

<u>Final Thoughts</u>:

While we are on the subject of energy boundaries and personal protection... there is something else which we need to mention. During our discussion of Polarity Scenario 6 we said that there was a real danger that the Straight Male would react aggressively towards any feelings of attraction they might experience towards the Gay Male. This is because both of their Khats are Yang, although the attraction is between the Straight Khat and Gay Ka.

Unfortunately, this often means that the Gay Male is on the end of some overt hostility and aggression from the Straight Male, and it is very hard to protect yourself from this kind of attack, because it can be both physical and psychic. There is one thing which you can do to lessen the impact of your polarity on the Straight Male. Basically, you get your Gay Ka to extend its energy field around your physical Khat body, which helps to camouflage it on an energy level. If you can do this, then the repulsion which the Straight Khat feels will be turned to attraction, aggression will switch to sympathy... in theory.

---

2   Although, their Kas are probably getting 'hit' anyway. I think that's one of the reasons they become so desirable to the collective mind, because they have so much psychic energy being directed towards them.

You see, there is one potential problem with this approach. If the Straight Male is screwed up about their attraction to your Gay Ka, imagine what might happen if they start to experience more obvious feelings of attraction on the physical level. However, the Yang / Yang polarity which was fuelling so much of the hostility will not be present, and the Yin Ka should be able to disperse much of the negativity. So it is not a fool-proof strategy, but it one which you can try, and if it works for the better, then use it... and if it doesn't then stop.

I will be showing how to do this in the Volume 2 PDF, along with some other cool energy techniques (see Appendix C on how to access and download). If you want to learn more about energy boundaries and personal protection, I suggest you also check out Brian D Parsons *Energy Boundaries* Volume 1 and 2, both available from Samarpan Alchemy Publications.

PART FOUR

There is some kiss we want with our whole lives.

Rumi

C25. Looking for an Established Lineage:

When a young spiritual seeker starts out on their quest for personal growth and enlightenment, then they are often given the following advice: *Look for an established lineage.*

This advice is usally based on the assumption that an established lineage:

- Has a proven track record lasting centuries or millennia.

- Has a good track record of helping individuals achieve salvation, enlightenment, moksha, or nirvana.

- Has a good track record of helping individuals cope with being alive, being human, and so help them to be happier, wiser, more loving and more compassionate individuals.

Back in the early 1980s, I once had a heated debate with a Religious Education teacher who argued that people should never look for answers outside of the religious tradition into which they had been were born. So if you had been born into a Christian family and culture then you should only seek out answers to your inner questions and desires within that particular faith and tradition. Ditto Muslim, Sikh, Buddhist, Hindu, Taoist, and Confucian.

His arguement was based on the belief that because established religions such as Buddhism, Hinduism, Islam, and Christianity have all been around for at least a thousand years, others longer, then over that time they have developed all the spiritual discipline and practices needed to a) keep people safe, and b) allow people to reach their desired destination. He also argued against people joining a cult, religious fad, or New Age system because of the very fact that it was new, so was untried and untested. To leave their birth religion put an individual at risk, because they were putting their life in the hands of unknown and untried spiritual beliefs and practices, in the hands of people who may not know what they are doing... or even worse, leaders who want to exploit their followers for their own personal gain.

Now, I am all in favour of keeping people safe, but I feel there are a few other things which need to be considered alongside his conservative arguments:

1) Many of these religions offer salvation after death... which is conditional upon following all the rules laid down in scripture. Seeing that no one has yet come back from the dead, the jury is still out on whether these types of religion are right and deliver what they promise. Until that happens, whether you believe in what they are preaching is still a matter of faith. Perhaps a better gauge of the effectiveness of any spiritual path is whether they make you more loving, more compassionate, happier and wiser in *this lifetime.*

2) An established lineage has to start somewhere. For example, 2,500 years ago, Buddhism was considered by mainstream Hinduism as a unproven cult and a dangerous fad... and people were warned against getting sucked in. If you follow the existing lineage argument, then none of the current religions would ever have got off the ground, because they all started as mavericks, opposing an existing tradition. If we followed the existing lineage arguement to its logical conclusion, then we should all be practising shamanism, the first and oldest spiritual tradition on the planet.

3) If a tradition has been around for 1,000 years say, then yes, it may have been tried and tested in the past, but is still relevant to the modern age? Culture, society and human consciousness is constantly changing, and what was right 1,000 years ago may not be *now*... especially if that religion refuses to update itself,

and clings to an ancient spiritual text as if it is law, for all time, and cannot be changed or questioned.

But these are just general problems, and when we start to consider the question of spiritual lineage from a Gay perspective we come up with a whole different set of issues and questions:

1) The majority of the existing spiritual lineages either don't rate homosexuals, or consider them to be an outright abomination. So how can you join something which condemns who you are? Well, actually you can if you suffer from guilt or shame, feeling that you are bad or wrong... ideas which were likely put in your head by the religions themselves when you were a small child. And none of these existing traditions have a valid answer to the question of why God keeps contnually churning out homosexual abominations for millenia after millenia.

2) If the spiritual lineage is prepared to accept you, then it is usually on *their* terms and not *yours*, and you will certainly need to change, behave or hide in order to fit in with the rest of the congegation.

And most importantly of all...

3) *There is no existing, established spiritual lineage which has been specifically designed by Gay Men and Women for Gay Men and Women.*

I might be completely wrong about that... There might be a secret valley up in the Himalayas somewhere, next valley along from Shangri-La, where Gay people have been secretly drawn to for centuries, and where they can practice a form of Gay Tantra in peace and total safety... Or maybe there is a lost tribe in Central America, where a hut is specially set aside for all the Gay members of the tribe, and the teachings of Gay Quodoushka have been passed down for countless generations... and fortunate Westerners are guided by signs and dreams to find their way to this lost tribe.

Maybe... But I doubt it. When you switch on your Internet search engine, and enter the keywords 'Gay Spirituality' what you see on the listings is, give or take, very much is what is available.

Now, I expect that you are waiting for me to say that I am hoping that Gay Polarity Tantra might become a valid spiritual tradition for Gay individuals, and my reply is yes, hopefully, but this is only Volume 1, and we are still in the early stages. I have thrown a few seeds out into the world, I have deliberately decided to start with the theoretical foundation and not the practical application, and it is still too soon to tell if any of this will take root. But for those of you who are looking for a spirituality which includes the Gay perspective, a form of Tantra that actively *includes* and *supports* Gay Men and Women, then I would humbly suggest you need to ask the following questions of any potential candidates:

- Is it practical?

- Is it safe?

- Is it inspiring?

- Can it take you outside of yourself and *beyond?*

- Is it grounded?

- Does it provide knowledge *and* experience?

- Finally, does it truly respect *who* and *what* you are 100%?

Because these are the very things which I am trying to establish within Gay Polarity Tantra.

C26. Gravity, Grace & Ecstasy:

The 20th Century mystic Osho used to say that there are two main forces acting upon human consciousness... the law of *gravity* and the law of *grace*.

What did he mean by this? Well, basically, all human beings live at the bottom of a gravity well created by the mass of our planet Earth. The Earth's gravity stops every one of us from flying off into outer space, which when you are trying to organise your life, get a good job and meet the partner of your dreams, would be a major handicap. I doubt you would get much done floating around in outer space, and breathing would be a definite non-starter. So, for our continued physical existence, gravity is a good thing.

In contrast, because Einstein says that mass creates gravity, which also has an impact on the space-time continuum, then you could also argue that we're 'trapped' at the bottom of this gravity well, which influences and limits our consciousness within a narrow band of space and time.

So when Osho is referring to the law of *gravity*, he is referring to the gravitational force of our planet which limits us, limits our energy field, narrows our mind, and tricks us into believing that we are nothing more than our mind, our body and our ego. In direct contrast, the law of *grace* is a counter-force, which lifts us up, widens our consciousness and our horizons, and helps us to see that we are so much more than our limited personality and physical body.

If gravity narrows our consciousness, and grace helps to expand it, than an interesting question to ask is 'What happens to human consciousness after it has escaped the gravity well of our planet?'

One of the things which NASA and the Russian space programme don't like to talk about much is the number of astronauts and cosmonauts who come back from their trip into outer space having experienced an altered state of consciousness. The most well-known of these astronauts is Edgar D. Mitchell, a member of the Apollo 14 trip to the Moon, who later founded the Institute of Noetic Sciences. Personally, I think that NASA and the Russians prefer their astronauts to come back as heroes, and not hippies.

According to the Institute of Noetic Science website www.noetic.org when travelling back to planet Earth, after having landed successfully on the Moon, Edgar Mitchell:

> Had an experience for which nothing in his life had prepared him. As he approached the planet we know as home, he was filled with an inner conviction as certain as any mathematical equation he'd ever solved. He knew that the beautiful blue world to which he was returning is part of a living system, harmonious and whole—and that we all participate, as he expressed it later, "in a universe of consciousness."

What I find most interesting is that, currently, there are a number of commercial enterprises who are competing to offer travel into space in the near future to ordinary people, which may be the start of something the press is calling 'space tourism'. OK, it will start with the rich and well-off, but as the costs decrease, than it may be possible for more and more lesser mortals to also take this trip of a lifetime. So what exactly is going to happen if and when more and more individuals escape the gravity well of this planet? What is going to happen if the human race ever starts to colonise space itself?

I have a feeling that maybe, thanks to space tourism, mankind may be on the brink of something *wonderful*. As more people get the chance to escape the limitations of this planet, and as hopefully the price of a return trip falls, so more people will get the chance to have their consciousness expanded. In a sense, they will boldly go where few members of the human race have gone before... journeying into *outer space* as a way to go deeper into *inner space*. And so the next big leap for mankind could be... ashrams in space! I bet that Yogic flying will be a whole lot easier in zero gravity...although you'll have to be careful not to bump your head on the ceiling.

A couple of years ago, NASA put the first married couple into space on the same space shuttle flight. During this trip, NASA went out of their way to stress that, even though they were married, and so could have legally engaged in sex during their flight into space, they would not be doing so. They would definitely *not* be the first members of the 500 mile High Club. Personally, I believe that was a great mistake by NASA, an organisation which must continually justify itself and its financial budget to the American taxpayer. If this couple had come back from their space trip claiming 'The sex in space is amazing. Best ever! You guys have got to try it!' I have a funny feeling that NASA's budget would have gone up tenfold in a matter of months, with U.S. Senators and Congressmen keen to explore the benefits of space tourism... for the betterment of human civilisation, obviously.

Across the centuries, mystics of many different spiritual traditions report that when they go into deep meditation there is a feeling of *expansion* and *weightlessness*, a feeling of being *lifted up*. This experience appears to be similar to achieving a state of internal weightlessness. Their meditation and spiritual effort has probably allowed them to tap into Osho's law of grace, which generates this feeling of expansion and weightlessness within them.

There have even been reports, sometimes corroborated by independent witnesses, of saints starting to float and levitate around their churches, such as the 17th Century St. Joseph of Cupertino (although it has never been possible to capture this on camera... maybe because they weren't invented and available in 17th Century Italy).

In everyday language, we commonly use expressions such as being 'down in the dumps' or being as 'light as a feather', and emotions are generally categorised as being either the high and uplifting variety (i.e. love, joy, bliss), or the low and pulling you down kind (i.e. depression, grief, hopelessness). So the concept of gravity and grace is woven into the very language we use when talking about our own feelings and experiences. The heaver we feel, the more depressed and trapped we believe ourselves to be and the less energy we have available to us. On the other hand, the lighter and more buoyant we feel, the more expansive our energy, the happier we are, and the more expanded our horizons.

So when Osho talks about the law of *gravity* and the law of *grace* then he is probably right, these two forces do influence our spirits, energy and emotions to a huge degree, either lifting us up or crushing us down. In Chinese energy medicine all of this is connected with the Triple Warmer meridian.

It is very interesting that one of the most popular dreams which people report is when they dream they are 'flying'... and the joy which they experience isn't that they are flying to *anywhere* in particular, there is rarely a destination involved in these dreams... the joy arises just from being weightless, flying for the sake of flying. When we dream we are flying then we experience a sense of ecstasy.

The original definition of word 'ecstasy' is important here. It comes from the Ancient Greek to literally 'step outside of yourself'. So, according to Ancient Greek mystics, when you learn to step outside of yourself, outside of your fears, guilt, shame, jealousies, anger, frustrations, and hate... when you step out of all those things which are holding you *down*... what you find, what is left, is a feeling of ecstasy. This is also interesting, because when we dream, we are less troubled by our everyday personality and its issues, so it is easy for us to connect with this state of inner ecstasy. So it appears being weightless and experiencing ecstasy is important to us on many different levels, in fact you could argue that it is essential to our continued health and wellbeing.

One of the reasons why some people choose to take drugs is probably to escape the crashing weight and pain of their ordinary lives, a temporary escape into a state where they feel lighter and freer. I am not saying this is the right route to take... but if you are experiencing unending, inner pain, then it is an understandable route of escape, and I have learnt that you should never sit in judgement over someone else's inner pain.

Now, earlier in this book, I said that we would be drawing upon two pieces of external information in support of the theory behind Gay Polarity Tantra. The first was the concept of the Khat and Ka, drawn from the Ancient Egyptian spiritual tradition. I shall now reveal the second piece of information, which is from Tom Kenyon's and Judi Sion's book *The Magdalen Manuscript*, where they include the following sentence:

> ... *The Ka is strengthened by ecstasy. Ecstatic states are nourishing and strengthening to the Ka body, and as I said earlier, with each strengthening of the Ka it becomes more magnetic, drawing to the initiate that which he or she desires.*[1]

According to Gurdjieff, another 20th Century mystic, everything needs food to exist. Our physical body needs physical food (i.e. grains, meat, fruits, nuts, and water), and each of our subtle bodies also needs food, although a different sort compared to our physical body.

It therefore appears that:

- Our Ka body needs love and ecstasy to survive and thrive, which kind of makes sense because it exists in a dimension of energy and so is not constrained by our physical laws. In other words, it would need a different kind of food.

---

1   Tom Kenyon & Judi Sion, page 37.

• Our Ka body probably doesn't appreciate being attached to the physical Khat body, which is itself trapped at the bottom of the Earth's gravity well. There are not that many chances to experience weightlessness and true ecstasy on the surface of planet Earth.

• However, there is always the option for the Khat to feed the Ka with the food it prefers, love, ecstasy, and every other positive emotion going. If the Khat can do that, then the Ka will start to fly, which will have the effect of lifting the Khat... and once the Khat is lifted, it will find it easier to access feelings of ecstasy and love, and so this provides the Ka with even more food, and so it expands and flies higher, which in turn... (I think you get the picture by now... the whole energy system takes off like a rocket).

Now, Kenyon's and Sion's book, and much of the important information contained within it, is based upon *channelled material*, which personnaly I don't have a problem with as long as the information presented is grounded, practical and relevant. But the great thing about this type of channelled information is that there are experiments and explorations which anyone can do to prove whether or not it is valid and useful information, regardless of its actual source.

From what Kenyon are Sion are saying, if the Khat knows how to send love to the Ka, then this strengthens the Ka, and the Ka is then able to help / strengthen the Khat. In fact, the best sort of food which the Ka receives is probably drawn from its own Khat. According to their book, that was one of the mystical traditions practised by the Ancient Egyptians. They knew that true ecstasy feeds the Soul.

However, this is where we come to another very, *very* interesting point. In *The Magdalen Manuscript*, a heterosexual couple, a man and a woman get together and engage in a tantric ritual, where his Khat helps to strengthen her Ka... because (as we saw in Energy Polarity Type 1) that is how their polarity works on the *archetypal level.*

Because a Straight Couple does not have a direct energy connection between their Khat and Ka (as shown in the diagram below), they are totally dependent on each other to complete the Figure 8 circuit and so circulate the energy between all 4 units and expand their energies.

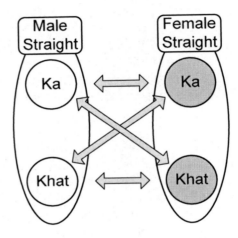

Figure 35: Straight Male & Female

But that is **not** the case for either a single Gay Man or a single Gay woman on the *archetypal level,* who (as we can see in the Energy Polarity Type 4 and 5 diagrams below) all have a direct polarity connection between their individual Khat and Ka.

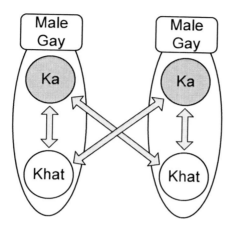

Figure 36: Gay Couples – Male

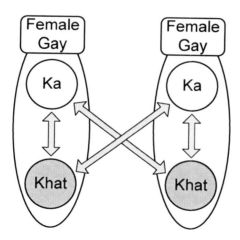

Figure 37: Gay Couples – Female

This means that it is hard for a lone Straight individual to engage in solo sexual cultivation… but very easy for a Gay individual to do the same... because their Khat and Ka is of opposing polarities, and so it is very easy for them to establish an internal flow of energy on the *archetypal level.*

And this is the really, really important thing... the Gay person does not even need sexual energy to achieve these benefits... and they don't even need to be in a relationship. All it takes is a little love from the Khat to start the energy ball rolling. All an individual needs to do is to learn how to set-up the energy connection between their Khat and Ka, and then start to share positive and uplifting energies with their Ka... and because the Ka is Yin in nature, it can magnify and expand these energies tenfold before transmitting them down again to the Khat.

Has anyone ever told you that an experience of love and ecstasy can be like sitting in the centre of fast breeder nuclear reactor? When the energy takes off... truly mind-blowing!

If we return to the concept of gravity here, Gay individuals appear to have their own inbuilt rocket system, which when 'activated' can lift them up above the heavy gravitational field of this planet, allowing them to easily experience the law of grace and true ecstasy.

In contrast, Straight individuals need a partner of the opposite sex to achieve the same result, and so it takes a little more organisation and effort on their part.

Gay individuals don't need a partner to help them reach these spiritual heights, but when they *do* find someone else, a same-sex partner who is willing and able to engage in this kind of energy work, than together they really can blast off into the depths of outer space.

This is also the complete opposite to Mantak Chia's belief that Gay people have to devote extra time and effort to gathering sufficient Yin or Yang from the external world to compensate for their not having a partner of the opposite sex. Within Gay Polarity Tantra all you need to do is cultivate an inner connection to your inner Ka, which is automatically the opposite polarity to your physical Khat. This is the advantage which the earliest Shamanic cultures were aware of many thousands of years ago, when they spoke about the 'two-souled ones'... and which the later Straight priests tried to crush and outlaw.

The advantage has never gone away. It belongs to Mother Nature herself, and so cannot be crushed or forbidden, whatever the Pope or priests might say or write to the contrary.

It's been buried and lost after 4,000 years of religious indoctrination. But it's still there, even now, within the energy system of every Gay men and women on the planet... just waiting to be re-activated and explored. Just waiting to explode into ecstasy...

C27. What is Sexual Meditation?:

Next, we need to consider the question, 'What is sexual meditation?' Or, put another way the question becomes, 'How can you utilise sexual energy within the context of meditation?' Is it even possible?

I mean, meditation is usually depicted as 'sitting quietly, observing the breath, allowing the grass to grow by itself'... while sex is meant to be all about passion, movement, deep breathing, with multiple limbs thrashing about all over the place. However... there are a number of spiritual traditions around the planet – Tantra, Taoist, Quodoushka for instance – which utilise sexual energy in *some* of their spiritual meditation practices, and claim that the union of the two is indeed possible.[1] But before we address the question of '*What is sexual meditation?*', first we probably need to start with a workable answer to the question of '*What is meditation?*'

Now there are many possible answers to that question... and probably every spiritual tradition which is currently in existence has a different answer for the aim, purpose and benefits of meditation. But the particular answer which we will be using in this book is based on the metaphor below:

> *Imagine you are living in a part of the world where it has been overcast for the past couple of months. Just grey clouds overhead, not a single glimpse of sunlight or blue sky for day after day after day... It has been miserable and depressing, and you need to do something to lift your*

---

1   Quodoushka is the form of Tantra traditionally practiced amongst the Central and Northern tribes of America, before the coming of the White Europeans. It has absolutely nothing to do with Quidditch from the Harry Potter novels, a form of basketball played on broomsticks... Although rumour has it that there once was an unofficial, sixth-form Tantric sex club at Hogwarts, long ago, in Voldemort's final year. Obviously Dumbledore wasn't allowed to join, because he was Gay.

spirits. So you decide to book a holiday abroad, somewhere far away, somewhere with bright sunshine and endless blue skies.

Finally, the day arrives for the start of your holiday, and you travel to the airport to catch your flight. You park your car in the long-stay car park, check in and then wait patiently in the departures lounge, until finally they call for your flight to board. You enter the plane, take up your window seat, and stare through the small, thick glass pane, as the plane starts to taxi along the long runway, and then turns for take-off.

As you look through the small glass window, you see that, even now, it is still raining hard outside, as the plane comes to a complete stop at the start of the runway.

... And then the plane starts to accelerate down the runway, with the engines on full throttle... faster, faster, faster... and then there is that strange feeling when the wheels suddenly leave the runway and the wings are lifting the entire weight of the plane... and the plane starts to climb upwards at an angle...

Going up... soaring up... up into the clouds.

For a moment, as you look out of the small window, all you can see is grey, depressing clouds pressed up against the pane of glass.

And then suddenly the plane breaks through the cloud layer... and brilliant, golden sunlight pours through all the small windows along the length of the plane, and the cabin is completely ablaze with light.

You see the blue sky and the sun above... and your spirits are instantly lifted.

It's amazing. In a matter of seconds, the world and how you feel has been completely transformed.

OK... so what does that analogy have to do with meditation? Well, let us suppose that we, the personality self, existing in our physical body, are living out our lives *below the cloud level*, a blanket of unbroken grey cloud. We have a vague sense that *above* the clouds there is an infinite blue sky of unconditional love, peace and joy... but it is up there, *somewhere*, although we cannot see it, let alone feel it.

Because there is this layer of unbreakable clouds continually above us, preventing us from seeing and experiencing the inspiring and uplifting blue sky we have been told about... and so for us, living below the clouds, life is a gloomy, grey and depressing affair.

We may have heard about the blue sky from others, read accounts of other people who have claimed to have seen it, but we ourselves have never experienced sunlight, seen it or felt the warmth of its rays upon our skin. And for some people, they doubt that it even exists.

So, in this metaphor, what do the clouds represent? Well... The clouds represent our mind... or at least our constant and continual barrage of thoughts and thinking. As an ancient Zen master once said 'Good thoughts, bad thoughts, it really doesn't matter what you are thinking about, the problem is thought itself.'

If I were to ask you **not** to think about a pink elephant, what happens... immediately the thought of a pink elephant pops into your mind... In fact, a whole heard of trumpeting pink elephants may even now be rampaging across your mental panorama... yes? If I ask you your opinion on a current political debate, and you say, 'I don't know, I have never really thought about it.' ...even then, thinking about something you have never thought about, sets off a new chain of thoughts.

The reality for the majority of human beings, during their waking hours, is that we are constantly 'thinking' about something. The things we like, the things we dislike, what we want to achieve, or more often what we definitely want to avoid. It's like a mental soap opera continually running in our heads, where we are both hero and villain. Basically, your average human being is pretty useless at **not** thinking, or at least surviving the odd minute or two without the need for thought.

Just imagine for a moment that you are sitting perfectly still, and for one moment in your life, you have everything you want and need, and have absolutely no worries or concerns at all... so, under these circumstances, where everything is just *perfect*... what would you need to think about? Nothing really... In that moment you would have it *all*, you would be perfectly content and fulfilled.

So, for that brief moment in your life, without any desire or need, wouldn't it be alright to just 'switch off' your mind, even if only for a moment or two.... give it a rest perhaps?

But do you even know *how* to switch off your mind? And even if you could, would you want to? Or would you be afraid that you can't survive without your mind being on constant alert, to help you with some unknown circumstance which might suddenly require the need for thought?

Your average human being is convinced that *thinking* is as essential as *breathing*, it is part of what a human being does... and as a result we have lost the ability to switch off our minds, even if only for a few seconds. We can't even imagine a life without thinking. Our education systems focus on helping us to retain information, and to think better and smarter. Not once are we ever shown where the mental off switch is located inside our heads. For the majority of human beings, their consciousness is simply drowning in an ocean of thought from childhood to old age.

So on our perfect day, we'd probably sit there, thinking about how perfect our life is... or maybe wondering if it could get any more perfect... or maybe worrying about when this moment of perfection will all end. Yes, there is a beautiful blue sky of unconditional love, joy and peace up there... but it doesn't live above us, but **within us**... and our constant thinking creates the barrier which disconnects us from experiencing this infinite sky within. The truth is *thinking* is our internal cloud layer.

I never understood what the ancient Zen master meant until I realised that mind and thinking is the mechanism which generates our inner mental clouds, which separates us from the wonderful spaces which lie within us... just out of reach. It doesn't matter what kind of thoughts we are thinking... good or bad... beautiful or ugly... they are all still thoughts, and it is only when thought ceases completely that the mental clouds clear, and we can experience our internal, clear blue sky. But the problem is that we are so used to 'being' our mind, that if we do happen to drift up above the mental clouds, and experience these states of love and bliss, even for a moment... we'll instantly think '*Wow, this is amazing!*', which is another thought, and this thought automatically pulls us out of the experience of ecstasy, and back down to the mental cloud level once again. You can either directly experience ecstasy with your mind switched off, or you can think about ecstasy but not experience it, those are the only two options available.

It is very hard to escape the trap of thinking... unless you learn to switch off the mind entirely. And that is what the aim of meditation is. The first of the Yoga Sutras of Patanjali states that:

> *Now the discipline of Yoga. Yoga is cessation of the mind.*
> *Then the witness is established in itself.*

When the mind chatter stops, then consciousness can rise up and appreciate the view *above* and *beyond* the mind. However, the vast majority of people are foreign tourists in this world of ours, too busy taking pictures of an ancient monument that they don't ever bother to take the time to actually *look at and appreciate the amazing reality which is right in front of them*. They are using their cameras to experience the world around them, and not their own eyes, and only really savour the experience when they are back home, looking at their photographs.

Basically, the mind can only function at the mental level, and *does not function at all above that level, and was never designed to*. This is why the mind cannot comprehend states such as bliss, ecstasy and unconditional love, which all exist on a higher vibrational level then the mind. All the mind can do is think about them, create mental concepts which are meant to represent these states of being... and yet, mental concepts are not the experience, and only exist at the same level as the mind, and so describe the experience second-hand. This is why in NLP (Neuro-Linguistic Programming) they say that the 'map is not the territory'. Language is not the experience... just words which describe and crudely communicate the experience to others after it has happened.

But we're so identified with the mind that we believe our consciousness can only go where our mind goes. This is not the case... because our consciousness and our mind *are not the same*. So, as the mystic Osho once said, 'The trick is to use the mind to go beyond the mind'.

Meditation is the ability to silence the mind, for a time, so that our consciousness can rise upward / inward into these expanded inner spaces, and not be continually dragged back down by our thoughts. You don't want to destroy the mind, because when you come back down to earth, your mind is still very useful, it helps you to navigate life, to get your needs met – i.e. shopping, driving, filling out your tax return, stuff like that. Instead, you need to develop the ability to switch off the mind for a time, and then switch it on again when it is needed.

So the next question, 'What is sexual meditation?' Well, the answer to this is quite simple. With sexual meditation you are using sexual activity and sexual energies to silence the mind. You are hoping to use ecstasy and pleasure to silence the mental chatter. And there are several advantages to the use of sexual energy in this context.

Firstly, pleasurable sex allows a person to focus their awareness in their physical body. It's like a magnet, it draws your consciousness within, and you are less distracted by external sounds and events. This brings your focus into the present moment.

Secondly, sex usually isn't boring (or at least it isn't if you are doing it properly). So it is something which many people will find more appealing than sitting silently, unmoving, on a meditation cushion for 1 hour a day (which to the uninitiated really does sound like total boredom).

The third, and probably most important thing, is that as the sexual pleasure builds, a point comes when the mind, all the mental chatter, completely *stops*... the mind just gives up, and you are just *peacefully* aware. You will have reached a space which is above the mental clouds, and can directly view the blue sky beyond.

But why should this be? Well, it is said that the conscious mind can only process 10 bytes of information per second, and most of those bytes are used up with mental chatter (sometimes politely referred to as our stream of consciousness). But as sexual ecstasy builds, and you focus your awareness completely on your physical body experiencing ecstasy in that moment, a point comes when our conscious mental mechanism can't handle any more information, and has no choice but to close down... it becomes overloaded with too much pleasure... which then allows your pure consciousness to expand upwards, outwards and inwards. It's a bit like a Zen koan but one in which sexual ecstasy, instead of an unsolvable mental puzzle, causes the monkey mind to close down.

And this is one of the things I believe the Tibetans may have meant by their spiritual phrase 'emptiness and bliss'. When the mind is empty, we can experience the bliss that lies beyond the mind. When there are no inner clouds, then we can stare upwards at the blue sky above. But to build up sexual energy to the point at which it overwhelms our mental chatter, we need Yin & Yang... but most of all, we need Yin.

A long time ago, I had a biology teacher who used to say, while she was teaching us sex education, that during sexual arousal, men are like *fire-lighters*, but women are like *forest fires*. Or put another way... men / Yang are quick to arousal, but also quick to burn out... women / Yin are slow to arousal, but once they are on fire, then they can burn for a very, very long time indeed (and so men had better be ready to handle that amount of intensity once it gets going).

So if you going to use sexual energy for meditation, regardless of whether you are Straight or Gay, you can only achieve the excessive amounts of ecstasy which can switch off the mind if you take the time to build it up to this same level of intensity. And for that you need Yin. Remember, Yang starts the fire, but Yin holds and intensifies it.

In addition, to use poetic language, the process is one of 'Yang surfing Yin into bliss'. And, to be honest, the process *is* a bit like surfing.

A surfer paddles out from the shore, and then waits patiently for a big wave to arise from the depths of the ocean. They wait a while, and then a big wave emerges, and the surfer gets up on their board, and rides the wave to shore... And then the process starts all over again, with the surfer swimming out to catch the next big wave...

In the bedroom, the process is the same. Yang starts the fire, Yin contains and intensifies it... but Yang has to wait patiently as Yin builds the waves of orgasmic energy... But when they come, they come first in steady ripples, and then larger waves, which then build and expand over time.

So it is a bit like surfing. You wait, you catch a wave, you surf, you swim back out, you wait, catch an even bigger wave, you surf, you wait, catch an even bigger wave, you surf...

But the last thing to consider is that final piece of information which we are drawing from the ancient Egyptian tradition.

The Ancient Egyptians used to believe that you needed to feed your Ka, which is why they would store food in their tombs, to metaphorically feed their Ka after death.[2]

Tom Kenyon and Judi Sion, in their book *The Magdalen Manuscript*, says that what really feeds the Ka is **ecstasy**... which is something the Tantric path delivers in spades.[3] It's a bit like those scenes in the Superman movies, towards the end of the film, where Superman has been weakened in some way, usually with Kryptonite, but manages to fly above the clouds (clouds again) to bask in direct sunlight, and in these movies our yellow sun strengthens and replenishes him. If we can lift our Ka into a state of ecstasy, then this will strengthen the Ka, and when our Ka is strong and healthy this feeds back down to us, the physical Khat, living out our lives below the clouds (mostly).

Now the next question we need to ask is, 'What are the *downsides* to all of this?' Usually there is a downside or three involved in such things... Yes, there are two downsides, but these arise *not* from the mechanism / process itself, but from the harm our culture and religions have done to the natural mechanism which resides within us:

------

2   There is one good thing you can always say about those Ancient Egyptians, they definitely knew how to plan ahead.

3   Although Tantra is not the only way to achieve this. I have found the light body path is also a great way to feed and strengthen your Ka with ecstasy. But you do need to consciously include it, or else the process doesn't work. You not only need to set a place for it at the table, you also need to remember to invite it over for dinner. For more information go to www. orindaben.com.

Firstly, back in the 1960s and 70s, when Western spiritual seekers first journeyed to India in search of a genuine spiritual master, the genuine spiritual masters which they found were totally amazed at how emotionally messed up all those young Western men and women were.

One such master has said, 'With Indians, all I have to get them to do is surrender their ego... but with these Westerners, first I have to help them *fix* their ego, which is in such a poor shape, an emotional and mental mess... and only *then* can I start the process of helping them surrender their ego. Working with Westerners involves so much more work. Because you can't surrender something you don't fully have.'

A similar situation applies in the Tantric sphere, Gay or otherwise. Our sexuality should be a natural gateway to pleasure and ecstasy, but because our culture, society and religions have spent the last 2,000 years demonising it, most people have layer after layer of fear, guilt and shame burying something which should be so natural and easy to work with. Nowadays any system which hopes to use sexual energy for spiritual purposes must start with some kind of 'archaeological dig', to uncover and remove all the layers of suppression and repression before it can help someone access and use the true potential which lies dormant within them.

But then, on top of this we must also consider that in his book *Arousal: The Secret Logic of Sexual Fantasies*, the psychologist Dr Michael Bader argues that in order for sexual energy to flow, an individual needs to feel safe, internally and externally, a state which he refers to as psychological safety. But if they do not feel safe internally, because of fear, shame or guilt, then the unconscious mind usually generates some kind of sexual fantasy, literally *a work around* which allows that individual to *feel safe*, and so express their sexual nature.

Normally, a person cannot feel sexually excited if they feel afraid. But if their unconscious mind can engage them in a sexual fantasy, which allows them to feel unafraid, then their conscious mind will feel psychologically safe, and so be happy to engage with their sexuality. Although to the outside observer, their sexual fantasy, and the way that individual chooses to express their sexuality, may be quite distorted, to the individual it makes perfect sense, and it is their way of dealing with, and getting around, all the limiting beliefs and emotions trapped within them. According to Bader, a person who is a masochist is probably suffering intense *guilt*, which would quench any sexual desire in a normal person. However, if their unconscious mind can link sexual desire with the idea that they have been *bad* and so need to be punished, then sexual desire will come on line once again.

In addition, someone who is a sadist is probably suffering from intense *shame*, but it is possible to get around this shame, and experience sexual desire, if the unconscious can create a sexual fantasy where that individual is *all powerful* and *in control*. This will allow them to feel psychologically safe enough to express their sexuality.[4] Bader believes that sexual fantasies shine a light into the deepest workings of the unconscious mind... although they are so private that normal therapists and counsellors are never allowed easy access to these areas by their clients... or only after years and years of therapy.

The problem from a spiritual sex point of view is that, for such clients, engaging in spiritual sex is a bit like pouring 'petrol on to the flames'. In a 'keep your clothes on' type of therapy session, the client might be able to hide their true sexual fantasies for years, but as soon as sexual energy is brought into the mix, these sexual fantasies will come surging to the surface, and need to be dealt with and resolved if that person is ever able to use sexual energy for meditation. Because if they don't, the sexual energy will keep them trapped in their fantasy, and so cannot be something they can use to take them into the moment.

If the individual is not prepared to face this side of themselves, process

---

4   It should come as no surprise that sadists and masochists are the perfect fit for one another. Someone who believes they need to be punished, and someone else who is happy to oblige.

and release it, which could be very hard for them to do because the original experience may be buried deep and be painful to access, then the possibility of using sexual energy for meditation will be *impossible*... because that individual will be lost in their own sexual fantasies. That is the thing about sexual energy... it can be used to set us free of our fantasies and inner bondage... but it can also be used to enslave us even further, to re-inforce our fantasies, and so make their inner bonds even stronger. Therefore, it is up to each individual to decide for themselves how they wish to use this most powerful force which lies within them.

And when the world is broken, hot and colder
No one ever knows the reason why
For the ones we may become
For the balance we have won
For the day we wish the sun
Gonna play it loud tonight

Take That
These Days

And if it seems we are near the end of this story, the truth is we have only just begun.

Peter Kingsley
A Story Waiting to Pierce You

Volume 2 & What Happens Next:

OK, that's it, apart from the Appendices, we are now at the end of *Gay Polarity Tantra* Volume 1.

Hopefully, I have now managed to map out the theoretical model for a viable form of Gay Tantra, and one which also outlines how the Gay polarity sits within (or next to) the polarity of our Straight brethren (or the heterosexual-homosexual spectrum as many sexologists prefer to call it).

Volume 2, which is available now to download for free as a PDF from www.samarpan-alchemy.co.uk contains extra supporting information, which it was not possible to include within Volume 1, along with practical energy techniques for you to work with and explore. Information on how to access and download Volume 2 can be found in Appendix C.

My plan is that a future Volume 3 will contain even more practical information, which will help make *Gay Polarity Tantra* a reality.

Volume 1 is the *why* book, and Volume 3 will be the *how* book... although Volume 2 contains a slice of the *how* as well... hopefully enough to wet your appetite and get you started in the right direction.

But, for me, this raises a very interesting question... because as I am currently writing these words, I have no idea what is really going to happen next with *Gay Polarity Tantra*. I have a few ideas... but will they pan out... who knows?

I know it works from my own experience, so personally I am happy and fulfilled... but will anyone else out there be interested in what I have written... and if they are, will that interest be sufficient that they also want to try it... will anyone be excited by what I am putting out there, and want to take it further?

As I write these words... *I have no idea.*

There are times when the Universe asks you to complete something, to bring something forth... and you are obliged to do it... whether to repay a karmic debt, or for the health and wellbeing of their Soul, or to benefit and further the collective. Actually, often it's a case of the Universe twisting your arm behind your back, and frog marching you in the required direction.

The writing of this book, the putting out of this information into the public domain is one such instance. I had to do it for my own personal karma, growth and wellbeing... but now that it is *done*, I am really not sure about where it goes next. But it feels like the answer to that question will largely depend on whether there are enough people out there who want / desire it to go further. So whether or not I write Volume 3 will depend greatly on the feedback I get from Volumes 1 & 2, on whether that feedback is largely positive, and whether people want to engage with the practices that will be contained in Volume 3.

I am not expecting the feedback to be 100% positive, supportive and glowing... I know how the human mind works, and I know that people always love to criticise and find fault.

But if after reading this book, if you want to tear it down because you dislike what it says... are you going to take on the task of putting something else in its place... or do you like being destructive because you have nothng better to do?

If you argue that this book is *wrong*, do you have the courage, ability and commitment to explain what is *right* and *why*... and *how* your system will help Gay people lead more fulfilled and happy lives? Because that's what I have tried to do here... so if you are going to rubbish my ideas, then I challenge you to come up with a theory which is as *good as* or *even better*, along with supporting evidence and practical applications.

Now, I can imagine someone else out there in Readerland thinking to themselves, 'OK, you have given us a lot of theory, some of which is very interesting, but I don't see how you could make practical use of it... I don't see how you can apply it.' This is a very good question, and one which I am happy to answer by saying the first tranch of practical energy techniques are contained in the Volume 2 PDF... and some of the Audio Essences relating to those techniques will be available to download for free.

Each of these Audio Essences MP3s contain vibrations which support a particular aspect and experience within *Gay Polarity Tantra*. You will also find some of these GPT Audio Essences are specifically created for Gay Men, while others are created for Gay Women (because there is a subtle difference in how the energy works and expresses between the two). So be careful to download the right one. Listening and working with these free Audio Essences should give you a good indication about whether *Gay Polarity Tantra* can offer what you are looking for.

Subjects covered in Volume 2 PDF include:

- Energy Work & Psychological Development
- Hot & Cool Sexual Energy
- Patience is a Virtue
- Practical Energy Techniques - Working with Your Khat & Ka

As I said earlier, information on how to download any of these MP3s or PDFs can be found in Appendix C of this book, but it does involve visiting www.samarpan-alchemy.co.uk.

Please be assured that the Samarpan Alchemy website is as secure and robust as we can make it, and the privacy of your personal details and emails are of the utmost importance to us. This information will **not** be shared with anyone else, and the will only be used by us in the future to marketing purposes.

If you do **not** wish to be contacted in the future, download the free MP3s from the www.audiohealing .co.uk website. Any emails stored from this site will **not** be used for marketing purposes, although that website does not contain the full range of free products which are also available from the Samarpan Alchemy website.

If you want to keep up to date with future developments in Gay Polarity Tantra, you can also choose follow to us on Facebook at:

- **Gay Polarity Tantra** (this is a closed group, and access is only permitted to people who have already downloaded the free Volume 2 PDF)

- **Samarpan Alchemy**

Thanks, Love, & Good Luck whoever and wherever you are, and as the Ancient Egyptians used to say:

May God go with you through all those dark places where you must walk.

Nathaniel Reeves
Devon, March 2015

If You Have Enjoyed This Book:

If you have enjoyed reading this book, then why not take a moment to give it a favourable review on Amazon or other retail websites, explaining what you found most helpful and beneficial, and why you would recommend it to others.

Any positive feedback you can provide is much appreciated, and helps support small independent publishers, such as myself, who rely on positive feedback and recommendations to get our work out to the world.

And if you have found any of the information in this book helpful, highlighting it becomes your way of passing it on to other people in similar circumstances (which is what good friends and neighbours do).

In addition, why not befriend Samarpan Alchemy on Facebook, and leave a positive recommendation there, along with any successes you may have had using these processes and techniques.

Thank you & Best Wishes!

Nathaniel Reeves
March 2015

Appendix A - Crystal Perspective Training:

Samarpan Alchemy currently offers modularised training courses based on the information and techniques contained within a range of Samarpan Alchemy books.

These courses are run via the school, *Samarpan Alchemy*, under the banner of *Crystal Perspectives Training.*

These courses are designed to help individuals:

- Change their perspective on life, and so change their life.

- Create strong and effective personal boundaries.

- Release thoughts, beliefs and emotions which no longer serve who they are *now.*

- Empower them with *new* thoughts, beliefs and emotions which are aligned to their ever evolving, unique personal path of growth.

We are deeply committed to providing students with a path of humour, commitment, integrity and trust. In return, we hope to attract students who are prepared to make a strong and serious commitment to their own personal growth.

If you have enjoyed any of our books, and feel that you want to take this work further and attend one of my *Crystal Perspective* courses, then we look forward to meeting you one day.

Please refer to the Diary page on our main website www.samarpan-alchemy.co.uk for information about the current courses on offer.

Appendix B - Other Samarpan Alchemy Publications:

Brian D. Parsons created Samarpan Alchemy Publications as a way to offer readers new perspectives on energy healing and personal development, along with information which is practical, beneficial and inspiring. We offer a range of publications, in both print and ebooks, and the list of titles currently include (by author):

Brian D. Parsons:

> *Energy Boundaries: How to Protect & Affirm Your Personal Space*, Volumes 1 & 2
> *Energy Astrology*, Volumes 1 to 6
> *Grounding (What It Is, Why It's Important & How to Achieve It)*
> *Really Useful Crystals*, Volume 1
> *Crystal Antidotes: Harnessing the Power of Crystals to Resolve Personal Issues*
> *Crystal Consciousness*
> *Lucid Manifestation: How to Really Feel the Feeling of the Wish Fulfilled*, Volume 1
> *Audio Essences & Crystal Holograms*

Nathaniel Reeves:

> *Gay Polarity Tantra*, Volume 1

Crystal Therapy Council:

> *How to Find the Right Crystal Therapy Course for You*

More information about current and future publications can be found at our main website www.samarpan-achemy.co.uk, and also within the free bi-annual, downloadable Newsletter & Catalogue.

Appendix C - Supporting Products, Free Material & The Samarpan Alchemy Newsletter:

Supporting Products:

Our books contain many practical techniques which you can use to ground and protect yourself, and develop and expand your personality, emotions and spirit.

Our books are therefore not just about theory, although that does have its place in helping you to understand exactly what is going on beneath the surface, but aims to provide you with a range of practical tools and solutions which you can use to improve your life and current situation.

Many of the techniques offered do not require you to acquire anything, and rely instead on your own ability to visualise, or repeat an affirmation, or alter the dynamics of an existing relationship, or use the abilities of your own physical body.

However, the remainder of the techniques in our books do require you to acquire or purchase 'something'.

Obviously, this creates a few potential problems.

Firstly, your current financial circumstances may mean you are unable to afford a long list of crystals or other protection / development devices... even though you may be in dire need of them.

Secondly, for those methods which do require you to purchase crystals / products, although a writer can endeavour to show you techniques and layouts which use easily available crystals, unfortunately, this is not always possible, and so you may end up on a quest to track down something which is not only rare, but quite expensive (which is the fate of people who come under the spell of some crystal books we could mention).

This has always been one of our main concerns. It's all very well putting information out into the public domain, but we believe that this information must not only be practical, it has to be also accessible, easy to implement, and it has to be as affordable as we can make it.

We simply can't see the point in teaching people a technique and then saying, 'But it's all academic, because you're never going to be able to obtain / afford the materials needed to practice it for yourselves.'

This is why, in addition to physical crystals, we also offer three additional vibrational methods as ways to practically work with the techniques we show you throughout our books. These three methods are:

• **Audio Essences**

Put simply, with an Audio Essence a positive vibration is converted into a digital sound file, usually an MP3 format, so that whenever you listen to that sound track you are also accessing the positive vibration which was originally 'recorded'... just through the act of listening. This is an Active method of working with these techniques.

• **Crystal Holograms**

Over the years, a number of different ways have been developed in which you can programme a distinct vibration into a crystal. The Crystal Hologram process, which we have developed, carries out the vibrational programming using a Light Life Ring™ and a laser.[1]

---

1   A Light Life Ring™ is a wonderful piece of vibrational technology discovered by a man called Slim Spurling. You can read more about him and these rings in *Slim Spurling's Universe* by Cal Garrison.

Using this method, the vibration which has been programmed into the Clear Quartz crystal is very 'robust and stable', when compared to other types of crystal programming, and can only be disrupted or removed through a clearing process which also involves a Light Life Ring and *two* lasers. Also, each Crystal Hologram is individually created, and not mass produced in some kind of 'energy copier'.

The Crystal Hologram is a Passive method, and so works without your needing to consciously do anything. It is therefore ideal to wear whenever you need protection or additional support while going about your day-to-day life.

• Energy Cards

Just as it is possible to capture, record and store a subtle vibration on to a sound file, or into a quartz crystal, so it is also possible to record and store these vibrations on to a piece of paper or card. When you do this, you create an 'Energy Card'.

An Energy Card is a Passive method, and so works without your needing to consciously do anything. It is therefore ideal to wear whenever you need protection while going about your day-to-day life. They are cheaper than Crystal Holograms, and so may be more affordable, and unlike actual crystals, they do not require regular energy cleansing.

Note: More information about Audio Essences, Crystal Holograms and Energy Cards can be found in the free *Samarpan Alchemy Supplementary Manual*.

As a way to make these techniques as accessible as possible, not only are we putting all the information about these techniques out into the public domain, we are also giving you a range of different ways to work with them.

This is how we can fulfil our own criteria – to ensure that each technique we show you is practical, accessible, easy to implement, and affordable.

If you already have all the crystals necessary in your collection to work with a specific technique given in this book, great, go for it... and you don't need to obtain or purchase anything else. Just use them in the way outlined in the relevent chapter.

However, if you do not have the required crystals... but you do feel drawn to working with any technique which you feel is appropriate to your personal circumstances, then you have the option to work with that technique either via an Audio Essence, or a Crystal Hologram, or an Energy Card... and so you can choose the method which you feel is most appropriate for your own situation and personal circumstances.

In addition, on our websites we also offer a number of free Audio Essences to allow you to try them out for yourself, and so test their effectiveness before you decide to purchase.

If you want to know how to acquire or purchase any of these products, then at the end of this chapter you will find a section on how to access and download the *Samarpan Alchemy Newsletter & Product Catalogue* PDF containing all the products relating to this book, as well as our other publications. This catalogue is constantly being updated with new items, and has a new article twice a year (1st January and 1st July), and so you are welcome to download it as many times as you wish or need.

Free Material:

To accompany this book, there is also a range of free material for you to download and play with:

1) *Gay Polarity Tantra*, Volume 2 - PDF

This contains a range of additional information about GPT, some of which it was not possible to fit into either *Gay Polarity Tantra* Volume 1, but which we are now providing to our readers for free. To download this free PDF, go to http://samarpan-alchemy.co.uk/ebooks.php and enter your name and email address, along with the ebook code, which for this product is:

FREEDOM1798

Once you click the Send button, the PDF will be automatically sent to your email account.

Volume 2 also contains a range of additional free products to download, along with the relevent codes to access and download them.

2) *Audio Essence - Optimism & Positivity - MP3*

This Audio Essence contains the vibrational signature for the Frequencies of Optimism and Positivity. To download this free MP3, go to http://samarpan-alchemy.co.uk/ebooks.php and enter your name and email address, along with the ebook code, which for this product is:

LITMUS1963

Once you click the Send button, the MP3 will be automatically sent to your email acount. This MP3 is 10 minutes in duration, and so should be OK to download into most email accounts.

3) *Samarpan Alchemy Supplementary Manual - PDF*

This ebook by Brian D. Parsons contains a range of supplementary information which will be useful to individuals new to vibrational healing, or who are just starting their journey of personal growth. It also contains additional information on Audio Essences, Crystal Holograms, and Energy Cards.

Because this information is useful to a number of different Samarpan Alchemy publications, it is has been placed into a separate ebook, and is available to download for free from our website.

To download this free PDF, go to: http://samarpan-alchemy.co.uk/ebooks.php, enter your name and email address, along with the ebook code, which for this product is:

URBAN7698

Once you click the Send button, the PDF will be automatically sent to your email acount.

The Samarpan Alchemy Newsletter & Catalogue:

As stated earlier, this bi-annual newsletter / catalogue contains the current product list for Samarpan Alchemy, and is updated with a new article on the 1st January and 1st July of each year. It also contains:

- A new article relating to some aspect of energy healing or personal development.

- Our current book list, as well as information about future publications.

- Our current live course schedule for *Cystal Perspective*

training.

This Newletter also contains our current distributuon websites and other outlets, so you can always work out which is the best place for you to purchase Samarpan Alchemy publications and products.

You are free to download this PDF as many times as you like, as well as distribute to your circle of friends.

To download this Newsletter PDF go to http://samarpan-alchemy.co.uk/ebooks.php and enter your name and email address, along with the ebook code, which for this newsletter will be the word NEWS plus the month / year in the following formatt MMYY.

For example, the code for the January 2021 newsletter will be:

NEWS0121

And the code for the July 2035 newsletter will be:

NEWS0735

Once you click the Send button, the PDF will be automatically sent to your email acount.

Important: If you accept to download any of these free products then you are also giving Samarpan Alchemy permission to use your email address for promotional purposes in the future... although Samarpan Alchemy will **not** share or sell on your email address to any third parties, and this information will be retained securely on our system. However, you always have the option to request that your email is removed from our lists at a later date.

Facebook & YouTube:

And finally, to keep up to date with the latest information, publications, products, releases, courses, and all other developments with Samarpan Alchemy, why not link up with our Facebook pages, **Samarpan Alchemy** and / or **Audio Essences**.

There is also a number of Audio Essences on **YouTube** which you may wish to listen to... so have fun!

About the Author:

Nathaniel Reeves was born in Devon, and studied for his first degree in London back in the 1980s.

He estimates that his subsequent and combined travels, and general wandering spirit, have lead to his circumnavigating the planet at least 3 times.

He is an accomplished energy worker, having trained in various forms of kinesiology, crystal therapies and light work.

Nathaniel can be contacted through our main website www. samarpan-alchemy.co.uk. He currently lives in Devon, having now returned from his many travels to the country, county and town of his birth.

Bibliography:

Bruce Bagemihl, *Biological Exuberance: Animal Homosexuality and Natural Diversity* (University of California Press, 2009).

Dr Michael Bader, *Arousal: The Secret Logic of Sexual Fantasies*, Virgin Books, 2003.

Cliiford Bishop, *Sex & Spirituality: Ecstasy, Ritual & Taboo*, Duncan Baird Publishers, 1996.

Valerie Books, *Tantric Awakening: A Woman's Initiation into the Path of Ecstasy*, Destin Books, 2001.

Amara Charles, *Sexual Practices of Quodoushka: Teachings from the Nagual Tradition*, Destiny Books, 2011.

Mantak Chia, *Taoist Secrets of Love: Cultivating Male Sexual Energy*, Aurora Press, 1984.

Mantak Chia & Maneewan Chia, *Healing Love Through the Tao: Cultivating Female Sexual Energy*, Healing Tao Books, 1986.

Tommy Dickinson, *Curing Queers: Mental nurses and their patients, 1935-1974*, Manchester University Press, 2015.

Gary Dolowich, *Archetypal Acupuncture: Healing with the Five Elements*, Jade Mountain Publishing, 2003.

Nik Douglas & Penny Slinger, *Sexual Secrets: The Alchemy of Ecstasy*, Destiny Books, 1999.

Nik Douglas, *Spiritual Sex: Secrets of Tantra from the Ice Age to the New Millennium*, Pocket Books, 1997.

Paul Ekman, *Emotions Revealed: Understanding Faces and Feelings*,

Weidenfeld & Nicholson, 2003.

Georg Feurstein, *Tantra: The Path of Ecstasy*, Shambhala Publications, 1998.

Mathew Fox, *The Hidden Spirituality of Men: Ten Metaphors to Awaken the Sacred Masculine*, New World Library. 2009.

David R. Hawkins, *Letting Go: The Pathway of Surrender*, Hay House, 2014.

Jeffrey Hopkins, *Sex, Orgasm and the Mind of Clear Light: The Sixty-four Arts of the Gay Male Lover*, North Atlantic Books, 1998.

Holger Kalweit, *Dreamtime & Inner Space: The World of the Shaman*, Shambhala Publications Inc., 1984.

Tom Kenyon & Judi Sion, *The Magdalen Manuscript: The Alchemies of Horus and the Sex Magic of Isis*, ORB Communications, 2002.

Peter Kngsley, *A Story Waiting to Pierce You*, The Golden Sufi Center, 2010.

Bruce Frantzis Kumer's book *Relaxing Into Your Being: The Water Method of Taoist Meditation Series, Volume 1*, Clarity Press, 1998.

Bruce Frantzis Kumer, *Taoist Sexual Meditation: Connecting Love, Energy and Spirit*, North Atlantic Books, 2012.

Hsi Lai, *The Sexual Teachings of the White Tigress: Secrets of the Female Taoist Masters*, Destiny Books, 2001.

Hsi Lai, *The Sexual Teachings of the Jade Dragon: Taoist Methods for Male Sexual Revitalization*, Destiny Books, 2002.

Stephen & Robin Larsen, *Joseph Campbell: The Authorised Biography*, Inner Traditions, 2002.

Stephen Mitchell (editor), *The Enlightened Heart: An Anthology of Sacred Poetry*. Harper and Row, NY. 1989.

Thomas Moore, *The Soul of Sex: Cultivating Life as an Act of Love*, Bantam

Books, 1998.

Virginia Nicholson's book *Singled Out: How Two Million Women Survived Without Men After The First World War*, Viking, 2008.

Osho, *Tantra: The Supreme Understanding*, Hind Pocket Books, 2011.

Osho, *The Tantra Experience: Disourses on the Royal Song of Saraha*, Thorsons, 1994.

Osho, *From Sex to Superconsciousness*, Harper Collins, 1997.

Brian D. Parsons, *Energy Boundaries: How to Protect & Affirm Your Personal Space, Volume 1*, Samarpan Alchemy Publications, 2015.

Brian D. Parsons, *Energy Boundaries: How to Protect & Affirm Your Personal Space, Volume 2*, Samarpan Alchemy Publications, 2015.

Daniel Ramsdale & Cynthia W. Gentry, *Red Hot Tantra*, Fair Winds Press, 2004.

Daniel Reid, *The Tao of Health, Sex & Longevity*, Simon & Schuster Ltd., 2014.

Diana Richardson, *The Heart of Tantric Sex*, O Books, 2003.

Joan Roughgarden's *Evolution's Rainbow: Diversity, Gender and Sexuality in Nature and People*, St. Martin's Press, 1999.

William Schindler, *Gay Tantra*, Xlibris Corporation, 2001.

William Schindler, *Essays on Gay Tantra*, Xlibris Corporation, 2000.

Mieke & Stephen Wik, *Beyond Tantra: Healing Through Taoist Sacred Sex*, Findhorn Press, 2005.

Master Chian Zettnersan, *Taoist Bedroom Secrets*, Lotus Press, 2002.

Index